Some People You Will Always Love

Also by Lynn Baskfield

The Rakhma Story:
Unconditional Love and Caring for People with
Alzheimer's Disease and Dementia
by Shirley Joy Shaw as told to Lynn Baskfield

Some People You Will Always Love

Finding

the Stories

that Satisfy

Your Soul

Lynn Baskfield

Baroness Press
Minneapolis, MN

Some People You Will Always Love: Finding the Stories that Satisfy Your Soul
©2002 by Lynn Baskfield

Published by Baroness Press
Minneapolis, MN
USA

Cover design by Sara Sinnard & Erin Scott, Sarin Creative
Book design and production by Liz Tufte, Folio Bookworks
Printed in the USA by Patterson Printing

"I Speak from the Wisdom of the Dark, Moist Places" previously published in *The Phoenix,* Volume 16, Number 1, under the title "Voices and Visions."

Quotes and background information about Chief Joseph and Merriweather Lewis from William Albert Allard, "Chief Joseph," *National Geographic,* March 1977: 409–434.

"The Giving Blanket" won national runner-up in the Soul Making Literary Contest sponsored by the National League of American Pen Women, Nob Hill Branch, San Francisco, CA, 1997.

ISBN 0-9700683-0-1

Some People You Will Always Love

Finding the Stories that Satisfy Your Soul

Acknowledgments

I want to thank each person mentioned in *Some People You Will Always Love* for giving me moments of soulful reflection and years of quiet inspiration; they are the heart and soul of the stories told here.

I would like to thank my husband, Bill, a creative and talented man, for inspiring me to reclaim my creativity. His many loves—theater, music, dancing, literature—whet my appetite for finding my stories and for delighting in the stories of others. Through him I had a glimmer of how the creative arts can bring people alive, and I remembered my own writing and dancing and plays made as a child and abandoned.

I declared 1993 my year of creativity without having a clue as to what that meant. Shortly thereafter, a client of mine, Jan Coleman, suggested I get a copy of *The Artist's Way, a Spiritual Path to Higher Creativity,* which I did. Julia Cameron, the inspired author of *The Artist's Way,* opened up whole new worlds to me. Through her tools and teachings I have completed this, my second book, and I teach others how to access their talents, passions and playfulness, their stories and their souls. I am in love with my work.

I thank Bonnie Simrell for inviting me to the sweat lodge in Colorado where I began to understand how to find my voice, and I especially thank my friend Liz Aronica, who is no longer here in physical form, but whose spirit continues to nourish me, for inviting me to her story party one cold November night.

I thank Liz Tufte of Folio Bookworks. Her love of books and her heartfelt attention to quality make art of her work. She has truly served me in bringing this book forth lovingly and professionally. Ginny Hanson, who did a preliminary edit when I first started this project, helped me tighten up the text. Maureen Meyer, my final copy editor and proofreader, lent her impeccable eye to critical details I might have let slip. I don't know what I would have done without Liz,

Ginny, and Maureen. I particularly acknowledge the generosity of my four friendly readers, Shirley Joy Shaw, Wendy Sharpe, Risé Kasmirski, and Heidi Record, for reading the finished manuscript from a reader's perspective and giving me constructive criticisms and unexpected words of encouragement prior to production.

In gratitude, I bow to storytellers the world over, who, from ancient times to the present, speak to the human heart. And I bow to each and every one of you who carry so many stories that heal and make whole.

Introduction

I am a storyteller. I am a coach who uses the soothing salve of story to help people deepen their understanding of what fulfills them and to encourage them to take meaningful action in their lives. I am a guide who accompanies people as they mine the rich ore of their own stories. I am a listener who listens for the gold. I am a seeker who is taught and touched by the truth of experience revealed in the stories people tell. I am a storyteller and so are you.

As a personal coach, I start with the premise that my clients are whole and well, equipped with all the wisdom and resources they need to live a fulfilling life. There is nothing to fix. There is only space to be made to focus on what matters. The client is given a sacred space in which to nurture the garden of his or her soul. One way for clients to nourish their souls is to find and explore their stories.

I used to be a hairdresser. The salon was a place of transformation. Not only did clients leave, week after week, transformed on the outside, but they left awakened to their inner beauty as well. One day it dawned on me that my scissors and comb were for cutting hair, of course, but more important, they were instruments that brought beautiful souls into my life, souls that told their stories and listened to mine. We taught each other about the wisdom and resilience of the human spirit. Several of the stories in this book were inspired by my salon clients.

I did not go to college right after high school, but earned my bachelor's degree one class at a time, eventually finishing graduate school, all the while working in the salon. My formal education drew me to doing other kinds of transformational work, work that provides avenues of deeper understanding which enable people to move forward in life in unprecedented, very satisfying ways. So here I am now, a coach, a storyteller, a writer, and an educator sharing some of the thoughts behind the making of this book.

With so much cultural attention on dysfunction and self-help, it is easy to think that we are always just a grab away from getting better. Then we get better and find there is further to go. But there comes a time, even if we have had some bad breaks in our lives, even if we have had dis-ease, that we notice we are whole, and perhaps there is nothing to be fixed. Perhaps we are healed, yet even so, life keeps coming at us with new nicks and scrapes, new challenges and changes. There is always more to explore, as distinct from always more to fix.

My friend Pat works with a group of engineers. Never having worked in an engineering firm before, Pat thought that engineers developed products by perfecting an idea into a precise drawing, which was then made into a perfect prototype and, from there, put on the market. Now, after seeing the experimental methods that are basic to creating new products—oh, maybe this material, oh, that didn't work, let's connect the fastener to the plate, what about not using a plate?—she finds the process more random, more exploratory. "That's how my life has always been," she says. "I'm an explorer meandering forward and discovering random opportunity."

We are constantly creating ourselves, discovering who we

are by being in the world. Maybe we don't always feel like healthy, functioning people, but we are "meandering forward." This is what it is to be human, to create a life. There is no precise plan. It can be scary to be well and whole, and yet not have it together like we think a truly functional person would.

I heard Sandra Cisneros interviewed on public radio. She has written several books and many volumes of poetry. Around the time of the interview, Cisneros had been chosen as one of *Ms.* magazine's "Fearless Women of the Year." "Me, I am afraid of everything," she laughed.

I bought her book *Loose Woman.* Her language is raw and passionate, honed like fine pottery, shaped into goblets and saucers, sturdy yet delicate. She writes about love and sex, black dresses and red pickup trucks. Like popping SweetTarts in my mouth, her words explode into my own experience. I am awake again. I feel something. I see my own passion and my own courage, the raw experience of my body and the sacred ground of my love held squarely and dangerously in the curve of her fearless expression.

We are all of it, fear and fearlessness. Ease and dis-ease. Clarity and confusion. We discover ourselves through our creative acts, through being in the world. Maybe we feel fear, but we rise to a challenge. Or we live a quiet life of attention and service. Or we make many mistakes and keep on going. The daily meandering forward expresses who we are in the world and the fear is in not knowing how it is going to turn out.

It is important to have a community that sees this and reflects this back to us. Otherwise we dwell in the outmoded perception that "I am fearful" means "I am not whole. I am in need of fixing." It simply means "I am fearful," and we go on, designing our lives with threads of beauty, ribbons of love, and raw materials we find along the way.

Indigenous healers knew this. According to Angeles Arrien, anthropologist, storyteller, and author, when someone came to an indigenous healer with dis-ease, the healer would ask these four questions:

When did you stop singing?

When did you stop dancing?

When did you stop being enchanted with the stories, especially the stories of your own life?

When did you start being uncomfortable in the sweet territory of silence?[1]

---

[1]Arrien, A. (1994). *Gathering Medicine, Stories, Songs and Methods for Soul-Retrieval.* Audio Tape. Boulder, CO: Sounds True Recordings.

first became interested in storytelling at my friend Liz's story party (see page 9). It was hard to find my own stories at first, although I knew they were there. The first story I unearthed was *I Speak from the Wisdom of the Dark, Moist Places,* which can be found on page 83. It tells about a journey on which I find my voice, the voice that tells the stories. After my journey, all the stories in this book came, and more. They are about my life and the lives of people I know. They have all touched me in some way.

Stories tell us about ourselves. From them we can learn what our passions are, our themes, our obsessions, and our essential values—if we're awake. Then, when life demands whatever it does of us, we may go forth, enchanted by our stories, into the unknown to meet our challenges, delight in the magic, wrestle with our losses, and design new futures.

The stories in this book are about returning to the enchantment of our own lives. They are simple stories of the day to day. They are explorer stories. As Pat says, "There is no time off. It is all here in the moment. Even the littlest things can make a big impact—if we're awake." If we're not, we wait for someday, hoping to understand, waiting to feel less pain, looking forward to the day it will all turn out.

We all have personal anecdotes, things we tell about,

things that happen to us. Often we don't see them as stories. "Nothing much happens to me," you might say. "I really don't have anything interesting to say. My life just goes along. It's not like yours where so much happens."

I say, "Your life is interesting too. It is full of stories." Things happen every day, and as you allow yourself to look, to exercise your story muscles, you will re-member your life. To remember means to put the members back together. It means to become whole again. There is nothing missing.

To remember your life through story is a very ordinary, very exciting process. I encourage you not only to ask the questions the story exercises in this book suggest, but also to get out your paints or buy some—even if you're "not an artist." Start singing along with the radio. Dance down the hall of your apartment building. Spend some time with yourself. All of the indigenous healers' questions apply to you. They can help you find your stories.

Your body was made to move, touch, taste, see, feel, laugh, cry, holler, breathe deeply, and love. Use your body to unlock your stories. Your body will release the stories carried in its bones, its blood, its strength, its injured muscles, its aches, its quickness, and its slowness. Your body will tell you because it is wise and it always tells the truth—if you listen.

If you don't listen to your body, you are not alone. Our culture does not encourage it. Our bodies may gently whisper, "rest," "stop," "get more exercise," "love me." We rarely pay attention, however, until they whop us upside the head. I call it two-by-four therapy. Our bodies scream "Burn out!" "Stroke!" "Deprivation!" When that happens, we can no longer do our jobs or tolerate our children or have any sense of loving compassion for ourselves. That's when our stories become high drama. We get so embroiled in hanging on by our fingernails that we cannot separate who we are from the soap opera of our lives.

A good story has a universal message. It may be light and humorous or deal with difficult subjects such as abuse or loss. A good story touches us somehow; someone or something is transformed.

Stories transform when we realize we are not our stories, but instead, learn from them about what it is to be human. Says Salmon Rushdie, "Those who do not have power over the story that dominates their lives, power to retell it, to rethink it, deconstruct it, joke about it, and change it as times change, truly are powerless, because they cannot think new thoughts."

We are timeless, endless beings, deeply alive and interactive with the circumstances of our lives. But we are not those circumstances, nor need we be defined or driven by them. Soul-satisfying stories surface when we separate ourselves from our drama. Stories that satisfy the soul give us access to who we are. Our bodywork and our inner work give us access to stories that satisfy our souls.

Your stories don't have to be literal. You may depart from verbatim fact to access the truth of being. In other words, use the truth of your experience, of how you look at the world so that there is a universal message. Re-create the scene, even if you don't remember the exact details. The story will take off on its own. The characters will do what they want to do. Go with that.

For example, you remember a blue cup in the china cabinet that stood in the corner of your grandmother's dining room. You can take the cup and create a story around it. Who drank from it most often? Tell about that person. Maybe there is a story in how the cup came here from Russia. Was the cup only for company? Tell about the company that came to Grandma's house. Did a lover drink from the cup? Tell that story. You discover a lot about yourself when you dive deeply into your imagination and allow yourself to be pulled along.

For some of you this may be like using a new muscle, familiar from childhood, perhaps, but long since neglected—probably pretty flabby by now. Going on these flights of fancy will bring you back to your life in a new way. You will discover the power of your own stories.

As you look at the details of things a little more—colors, voices, mustaches, the texture of denim—you will begin to include them in how you see and say things, in how you reconstruct what your life is about. Tuning into stories that satisfy your soul is like getting a big screen color TV when all you've had before is a 13-inch black and white.

Use the exercises at the end of each chapter to find your stories. You are a storyteller. Your stories are powerful. Your stories will come.

Take to heart the words of Barry Lopez in his book *Crow and Weasel:* "The stories people tell have a way of taking care of them. If stories come to you, care for them. And learn to give them away where they are needed. Sometimes a person needs a story more than they need food to stay alive."[2]

---

[2] Barry Lopez, *Crow and Weasel.* San Francisco: North Point Press, 1990.

I

Finding Your Stories

Have you ever heard of a found poem? A found poem is made up of random words or phrases you find somewhere in your daily life, like on store signs, the names of fish lures, or in snippets of conversation overheard in a restaurant.

I found the following poem by putting together headlines from the August 26, 2001, travel section of the *Minneapolis Star Tribune*.

Win a Free Vacation

Harley's 100th will be hog heaven.
Those who give up seats earn rewards.
Too much football? No such thing.
You can fly! You can fly! You can fly!
Tango tells tale of seduction,
It's a sad feeling you can dance.
International SOS:
Rooms harder to find.
Hey, what's that?
Versace mansion to become hotel.
Fine art, fine beef,
Summer may be ending.
Upper Peninsula Fall . . .
This kind of magic is priceless.

To construct a found poem requires a willingness to allow something to emerge from what, at first glance, appears ordinary or unrelated. Finding your stories requires a similar kind of openness to the details of your life. If you let them, things will come together in fresh ways when you begin to look.

Sometimes, at first, what comes together might not make

much sense. That's okay. Let your creative side open to those non-linear leaps. That is called playing. We did it as children. For our stories to come tumbling back to us red-cheeked and excited, it is essential we be willing to play with them now.

The "Finding Your Stories" exercises that follow each story in this book encourage you to play with your life one question at a time. Each question has the potential to bring forth many stories, depending on how you look at it, depending on the person you are sharing with. Just as looking through the lens of a camera focuses your awareness on framing the picture within the whole, the exercises in this book help focus your awareness on snippets of experience that can frame your stories. Right now you are concentrating on finding the elements that resonate with you. To my mind, that is the most important thing. Later you can consider the ins and outs of how to craft them into powerful pieces.

"Story Seeds" is a game anyone can play that makes spontaneous storytellers of us all. I often play it in my workshops where there are several people, but you could play it with just two people if you don't have a whole group nearby. Here is how it works:

One person starts by giving a word to the person on the left. It has to be a concrete noun like *bird* or *hell* or *window*—not abstract like *love* or *beauty*. The person who has been given the word then recounts a memory or an image that the word stimulates. Responses can range from hilarious to touching. This exercise is juicy. Hang on for the ride.

To illustrate, one time someone gave me "poison ivy." Here's what popped into my mind:

A few years ago, my husband and I rented a cabin at a cozy little resort. Apparently the full moon that weekend made us giddy and we decided to make love on a blanket by a secluded lake across the road. In the shadows we spread a blanket over what we thought was grass. A few days later Bill's knees began to itch. You can imagine where that story goes . . . I get the giggles even now.

Someone else got the word *curve*. A moment's thought brought her to a curve life had thrown her when her daughter almost died from a heroin overdose. We felt her pain as she shared her story.

The key to "Story Seeds" is Do Not Censor!

Do not sit there and think about the right thing to say. Do not try to look good. Let the story that finds you come forward in its raw humanity. The real stuff is the good stuff.

You might also work with collage to find your stories. Give yourself 20 minutes to rip pictures that appeal to you from old magazines. Then take another 10 minutes to glue them to poster board. When you are done, make up a story about the images. It's best to do this quickly, before the mind begins to censor. Another approach to collage is to start with a question like "How do I see the opposite sex?" or "What is it to be grown up?" Rip images, and create a story from that. Or you can take a deck of tarot cards, shuffle them, choose a few to lay out, and make up a story.

In *Storytelling & the Art of Imagination* (Element, Inc., Rockport, MA, 1992), Nancy Mellon helps readers evoke nourishing, archetypal stories through the use of imagination and visualization. You may find yourself creating "storyscapes" that reveal lost parts of yourself, take you to a kingdom where wishes come true, or awaken you from the enchantment of a mean old witch.

Other people's stories may engender discoveries of their own. Before publishing this book, I asked four "friendly readers" to peruse the manuscript and give me their honest responses. Along with great constructive criticisms that made the book better, I was struck by musings scribbled in the margins. For example: In "The Package that Came for

Shirley" (p. 115), my friend Risé penned, "I long to find *my* grandmother's ring that is lost somewhere in *my* house." After "Just Dorothy" (p. 215) Risé wrote a note that could unfold into a stirring story of her own: "I had such a moment with *my* mother 12 years ago when I was in the thick of chemotherapy for breast cancer. It is one of the most important and sweetest moments of my life."

When you read or listen to the stories of others, notice what resonates for you. Because a good story has universality, because it speaks to the human spirit, other people's stories may become your own. Even the smallest point may touch you, as happened with an elderly woman who, after hearing a story that briefly mentioned a small-town blacksmith, was brought nostalgically back to the sounds and smells of the blacksmith shop in the small rural town where she grew up.

In addition to the stories of your own life, you may begin to collect stories that touch your heart or stir you in some way. Of course these are your stories too. And as the passage from *Crow and Weasel* I referred to at the end of the introduction suggests, we don't find our stories by straining for them. Instead they come to us if we are open.

For example, when I was in Todtmoos, Germany, to

attend a five-day Spiritual Emergence Conference, I had lunch with a woman who told me the most compelling story about forgiveness that I have ever heard. She recounted her experience of traveling through East Germany to the concentration camps of Auschwitz, Poland, and back again on the train the weekend the Berlin Wall came down. The story was so remarkable that it found both of us; me, for the first time, like a lightning strike, and her, with an impact of heightened awareness in the retelling. I have been savoring the story since, with the intention of sharing it in another book. It has touched me so profoundly I have had to hold it in my heart for a long time in order to appreciate its integrity and find a way to share its fullness.

Stories are all over the place, like pebbles on a beach. Start looking and you will find the pretty ones, the unusual ones, the extraordinarily ordinary ones, the ones you want to polish and take home with you. Your life is full of raw beauty. To find your stories, be willing to become enchanted again with your passions, your obsessions, your unfinished business, your deepest soul. Notice. Allow. Savor.

In this section, "The Storytelling Party" and "I Speak from the Wisdom of the Dark, Moist Places" speak to how I began to find my own stories. Although most of the others happened before "Storytelling Party" and "Wisdom" were written, I found them, waiting, after I realized that to find my stories I had to be willing to give them away.

The Storytelling Party

"I rented a storyteller at the Zen Center silent auction last night." I could picture the sparkle in Liz Aronica's gray eyes as she spoke breathlessly into the phone. "I'm going to have a storytelling party! The storyteller will be there and all our friends can come. You can come, can't you?" She gave me the details. I checked my calendar and promised to be there. It sounded like fun. Gathering to tell stories seemed familiar somehow, though I had never done it before.

An icy November wind chilled the evening, but the flicker of candles and a roaring fire warmed Liz's living room as we stepped inside, hung coats, and removed snowy boots. Dishes of homemade pasta, a few organic creations, some chicken wings, plates of cookies, and hot mulled cider provided by the guests brought everyone together in a toasty cluster around the sturdy oak table. We milled around for some time, meeting new people and talking to old friends. Then we gathered in the living room to listen to the stories.

Liz's living room was furnished with one cavernous rocking chair, a desk, the legless seat of another chair, a huge red and orange area rug, and lots of brightly colored, oversized pillows. Books lined the wall. Plants hung in various stages of well-being, some struggling for their lives. People settled onto pillows or perched on chairs imported from the dining room. Michael O'Neal, the storyteller, sat cross-legged on the floor next to Liz. Faces glowed expectantly in the candlelight.

Michael is a quiet, unassuming man, beanpole tall with a serene face and dancing eyes. He started out with a short story about a man visited by a stranger. It couldn't have taken more than three minutes, but it was a powerful story. Afterward there was silence, which Michael allowed to be without breaking it. Finally he asked us, "Who do you know who tells stories?"

It seemed we all knew someone.

"My aunt told stories every year at Thanksgiving. We know them by heart after all these years."

"My brothers told ghost stories around the campfire in the summer up at the lake."

"Every night before bed my dad told me stories about when he was a little boy."

"Garrison Keillor."

"My mother fled the Nazis with me in her arms when I was one year old. That's the part of the story I know. But I don't know the rest of it, or what's in my mother's heart, or how exactly my father died. I have dreams that make their own stories."

Everyone in the room became a storyteller that night. Michael never said another word. There was a story about a bus that broke down on a lonely road in Mexico. A story about a shaman's journey to the underworld. A story about tap dancing lessons and one about house guests from hell. Once in a while Liz would clunk another log into the fire or someone would tiptoe out to the dining room for more cider and I'd remember where I was, but the stories kept coming and people kept listening, absorbed and content until the wee hours of the morning.

It was good, Liz and I agreed the next day. We had

become best friends over the years of collaborating on a seminar called "Feeding the Woman in Ourselves," an intensive program for women with food and body image issues.

Liz was four-feet-ten and three-quarters and I am five-feet-nine. Before we worked together doing groups, I was her haircutter, and in the salon we always talked about things that mattered to us. Liz was a psychologist, and I was getting my degree in communications. I already had an extensive background in group dynamics. In the process of my education, I had developed a prototype for the "Feeding the Woman in Ourselves" workshop. During one of Liz's haircuts we got to talking about body image.

"Liz, I've always thought of you as the perfect woman. You're petite with exquisitely fine features, dark shiny hair, lots of life. You are beautiful. I've always felt too tall and too fat. I wish I looked like you."

Liz was aghast. "You're kidding, Lynn. I've always felt like I'm too small and too skinny. I've always looked at you and thought, 'Lynn is tall and graceful. She's beautiful. That's how a woman should look. I would like to look like her.'"

We drew in our breath; we could see the beauty in others but not ourselves. We each felt we alone lacked. But as we talked we noticed that although we each knew many, many beautiful women, we knew no one who liked her body the way it was. We wondered if it was because few of us are magazine model perfect that we don't celebrate and love our bodies. We realized that many women, including ourselves, had become disembodied, and that not claiming our bodies as our own causes great silent suffering.

That is when Liz and I decided to work together. We were perfect examples of how uneasy women are with their bodies, and I always teach best what I'm still learning. We spent eight years like Mutt and Jeff, doing our program through Liz's psychotherapy clinic and around the state for schools, clinics, and other organizations. We worked well together, growing ideas and and cultivating them like good gardeners, neither of us jealous or competitive, but truly working in partnership. One of us would develop an idea, the other would run with it for a while, we'd bounce it back and forth, and it would soon become a strong new entity with a life of its own.

We not only worked together, we floated down the Apple River with our kids together, we advised each other on how to raise teenagers, we went to funky Uptown restaurants now and then. We helped each other write personal ads and get through the times we spent with men and without them.

We wondered about the bigger questions of life like, Why are we here?

We grew to love each other. Neither of us had had a best friend since high school. It was fun to have one—me at age 39, Liz at 49.

The November after the storytelling party I had to appear in conciliation court over a sewer line dispute. I hadn't a clue as to how to handle the situation. Liz called and said she'd like to go sit with me in court, just to be there. It was something I never would have thought to ask her to do, but I was touched and relieved to have her with me. While I waited my turn in the hard pewlike benches in the back of the courtroom, Liz whispered to me, "It's been almost a year since the storytelling party. I think we should have another one. Do you want to do it with me?" Light streamed in from the window high on the wall behind us, softening Liz's pink lipstick when she turned her head and bringing out the purples in her paisley shawl. "I'd love to," I whispered back, taking comfort in having something to look forward to besides the next confrontational half-hour in court. "Deal. Let's do it—end of the month." The light played in Liz's silky black waves, creating a sort of halo effect. I could always count on her to remind me of the sweet continuity of life.

The next day the telephone rang. "Lynn, it's Don." Don was Liz's boyfriend. He never called me. "Liz died last night."

"What?" I screamed into the phone. "What??!!!" Through sobs that seemed like someone else's, with a voice not my own, I managed to ask, "How?"

"Asthma," he said. "Another one of her attacks."

Liz's bad attacks were maybe three or four months apart, but each one had been getting worse. She made light of them and got right back on her feet. The last two times she had to be hospitalized. This time she didn't make it.

"Oh my God. Oh my God."

"Katagiri Roshi came to sit with her. She would have wanted that."

"Yes." Katagiri Roshi was the abbot of the Minnesota Zen Meditation Center. He was Liz's teacher and friend.

I don't remember very much about the next few days, other than deciding to go ahead and plan the storytelling party. It seemed fitting and important. I held the gathering in my living room about two weeks after the funeral. A lot of people who knew Liz came to tell stories about her in the candlelight.

Stories heal the heart. They reveal something about being

human. They personalize life, yet make it bigger than our little griefs, our little victories. Tellers and listeners make community where each person in his or her own way learns, laughs, thinks, grieves, and grows. The stories about Liz brought her back to us and made us smile, yet they helped us release her a little more that night so we could go on with our own lives again.

Liz gave me my life as a storyteller. Almost every year since her death I have had a storytelling party. One year I had a theme: Stories of the Dark. Judy recounted a story about being lost on a camping trip in the dark. Dorothy re-created a car accident she witnessed downtown in the dark. Someone else shared a "dark night of the soul." One person told a ghost story, and another, a sweet story about dark molasses cookies.

Most of the time, a theme emerges, whether we start out with one or not. People bring prepared stories, but usually one story reminds someone of another story, and they just flow like they did that first year at Liz's. One year people told outhouse stories, another year, invention stories. Always, there is give-and-take and the stories are as unique as the individuals telling them.

My interest in storytelling has gathered momentum since

Liz died. I have taken storytelling classes from Maren Hinderlie at the Guthrie Theater and Jim Stowell at the Loft. I go to the Northlands Storytelling Conference in April, where storytellers from five states tell for three days. I tell stories now and teach about telling stories. It's a hands-on art that belongs to everyone.

One of the things Liz and I discovered back in the seventies and eighties when we were doing our "Feeding the Woman in Ourselves" workshops is that eating disorders, whether they result in obesity, weight loss, or closet behavior with no visible weight problem, are caused by a spiritual starvation that no amount of attention to diet will alleviate. There is an emptiness that cannot be filled with food. However it must be filled, and that is the challenge of recovery.

Barry Lopez, in his book *Crow and Weasel,* says:

"I would ask you to remember only this one thing. The stories people tell have a way of taking care of them. If stories come to you, care for them. And learn to give them away where they are needed. Sometimes a person needs a story more than food to stay alive."

There is an emptiness where Liz used to walk the earth, a place where she no longer is, a house that now belongs to her son, David. But it is a sacred emptiness—full with her stories and my own, with the questions we would endlessly ponder, full with the laughter and the tears we shared. There is a seamlessness that is undisturbed by Liz's departure, for her spirit continues to fill the spaces that cannot be filled with things. Liz, with her gentle wisdom, her attention and care, took me by the hand to feast from a bountiful table.

The Storytelling Party

Finding Your Stories

1. What storytellers do you know? What are some of the stories they tell? Retell the stories you remember, even if you don't remember them very well. Make up what you don't remember. Make it a new story. Make it your story.

2. When you tell a story, see yourself as a vehicle, a conduit for the story. Put yourself into your story by letting go, having fun, bringing feeling, and at the same time, get yourself out of the way. When you tell a story, give it as a gift.

3. Throw a storytelling party. Leave it open-ended or have a theme.

4. Find a book of stories or a tape of stories that interest you. Read stories. Listen to stories. Choose a story you like and make it your own by reading it over and over. Tape it and listen to yourself reading it while you are gardening or making dinner. Become familiar with the key concepts, important images, key phrases.

Don't worry so much about every word. Absorb it into your bones. Tape yourself telling the story without looking at the page. Or tell it to the mirror, to your child, or to a friend.

5. Tell your children or someone else's children stories about when you were little.

A One-Woman Wimbledon

Our program started with poems of loss and grief, moved on to that cocoon time of floundering in the dark, of not knowing what's next after a divorce, and ended with poems of new beginnings, new sense of self, new flight. I was surprised at how popular our poetry readings were with singles groups, since I don't think of listening to poetry as something a large group of single people out for a good time on a Friday night would be likely to do.

At first, the men and women in our little writers' group met privately to encourage each other's creative expression. Sharing our heartfelt poems, we soon discovered, not only gave us delightful creative outlets, but provided deep healing as well. Eventually, one of our members noticed the distinct stages of growth and change our writings expressed, dubbed us "The Butterflies," and started booking us for poetry readings with singles groups.

After our reading this particular night, a few of us Butterflies decided to join our audience at a local club for dancing. We sat in the good company of new friends, listening to music and drinking wine. I felt happily mellow and could have spent the whole evening just basking in the ambience. Then Pete asked me to dance.

He was dark and handsome and looked like my former husband, whom I hadn't seen or heard from for ten years. I really only wanted to dance, but a flood of feelings rushed in as I waltzed with Pete, all the unresolved longings for continuance or closure, all the dread that comes with being vulnerable. Pete and I danced the rest of the night. When he left, he didn't say good-bye.

I went home feeling empty, having opened that floodgate that I had so carefully dammed, even as I had resurrected my life and flown on sure wings to new places of growth and self-discovery. The place of partnership and love, however, was still a mystery, still a place of darkness.

The next day I lay down for an afternoon nap in my third-floor loft. As I drifted off to sleep, wedding bells chimed jubilantly from the church behind my house. I thought muddy thoughts about marriage, the bells more real than any wedding vow. I had been married in that church; I remembered my dress, my satin shoes that didn't make me taller than my new husband. I ached for something lost. I ached for what could never be healed.

I slept a deep, monotone sleep, flat black, like falling into an inkwell, when suddenly the door at the bottom of the stair opened and my twelve-year-old daughter Shannon called up to my room, "Mom, I know we're not supposed to bother you when you're sleeping, but . . . Dad's on the phone. He wants to take me and Louise out to dinner."

I leaped up. What? Dick lived in Missouri. Dick did not respond to phone calls or letters. Dick was unreachable. Dick might as well have risen from the dead as be on the phone. This must be a dream. "Shannon, you and Louise decide what you want to do," I said, still bleary and deeply shaken, knowing she and Louise were shaken too. A little later: "Dad is coming to pick us up in an hour."

What would I say to him? How would I be? I wanted to be there for Louise and Shannon too, but I was numb, I was a mess. The divorce had been ragged and bitter, with no resolution. I had been wife and mother, married at eighteen, divorced at twenty-four with two children. All my ideals about love and marriage had been shattered. There was another woman and, as is often the case, by the time an affair ignites, it is too late to address the real causes of stress in a marriage. All my anguish centered around betrayal, of having felt fooled, humiliated, and left to raise two daughters. I didn't know what I would say to Dick when he came.

I walked around like a zombie. I wandered outside into the yard. I stood there for a while. I pulled some weeds. I looked at the condition of the aluminum siding on the house. I lay down on the grass in the middle of the front lawn, drawn like a magnet to the earth. Gravity pinned me and held me. Time did not exist. Shirley, who lived downstairs, came home. Curious as to what I was doing lying spread-eagle on the lawn, she veered over to me from the sidewalk. "Dick is coming over in an hour," I said. She seemed so tall looking down at me, the sky behind her. She had been one of my main supports during the divorce. "Holy shit!" she said, and went in the house, leaving me glued to the grass.

After a while I heard Dick's pickup pull up to the curb, and I saw him get out. I pried myself off the ground. He looked older but so familiar. "Welcome," I murmured, and embraced him. That surprised me. I showed him into the house where the girls were. Cautiously, he hugged them and they him. He cried. They cried. I cried. Then they piled into his truck for dinner at Perkins. As if coming off novocaine, I began to feel again, little by little. I had the house to myself until they came back a couple of hours later. Before he left, I asked Dick if he wanted to join us for Sunday dinner. He did.

Time is a funny thing. Sitting around the table, the sound of silverware on plates, the smell of chicken, it was as if the four of us had done this yesterday, not ten years ago when Louise and Shannon were in high chairs. I felt like Tarzan ricocheting between past and present on a precarious vine, "Aaaaayyyyyeeee" reverberating through every cell, all the while buttering a baked potato and making small talk. Unreal. Surreal. A curse. A gift. Maybe I could bring my past with him to a close with some civil conversation, even some honest sharing, and go on with my life. After dinner, when Louise and Shannon left the table, Dick and I were alone.

"I've been wanting to be back in touch for so long," he said. "I got to thinking after my friend Bernard's son died, how he would never see his son again. They had never gotten along very well, but shortly before the accident, they had made peace with each other. Bernard had been real happy about that; you could see it on his face. After the accident— no more chances. He'd come over to my barn at night feeling so bad, he'd just walk around with me while I fed horses.

"I have daughters. I don't want to miss their lives. I feel bad about not being with them. I haven't known how to make that phone call. When they were little, I felt it was better to leave them be, to not complicate things. Besides, it hurt so much when I saw them and had to leave them off at the end of the day. Now, I've been wanting to call. Every time I come up to Minnesota for a horse show, I think about making that call. Then when I don't, I feel awful. Last trip up, I cried halfway back to Missouri because I couldn't pick up the phone."

"I don't know how they will be now, Dick," I said. "They have needed you. They have missed you. They love you and they are angry with you. I just don't know what to expect."

We sat down in the living room, Dick on the sofa and me in the wingback chair. We talked about a lot of things: memories, regrets, the lives we had lived over the years since our divorce, dancing. Dick had not danced much since we split up. He missed that.

He was still with Barbara, the woman he had an affair

with while we were married. It had been a rocky relation-ship, according to him. Sometimes they separated for several months at a time. They had never married, but Barbara had moved with him to the farm in Missouri where he built a horse-training business, and they made a workable peace with each other. "It's convenient," he offered.

"God spare me from staying in a relationship out of convenience," I replied. "That is my worst nightmare. It is how I felt when I was with you. After the kids came and I needed more from you, it wasn't convenient anymore and you were out of there. That's why I think I've never wanted to remarry. I won't be a convenience."

"I had a lot of big ideas then," he replied. "I was going to be the world's top horse trainer. Nothing was going to get in my way. I loved you, but I loved my work more. I let the marriage slide. Instead of listening to you, helping you, finding out what you needed, I felt dragged down. It seemed like Barbara understood. I'm sorry. I hurt you. I hurt the girls. I'd do it different today. But that's experience for you."

At the end of the weekend, we had talked more than we had talked during our whole marriage. When Dick loaded up his horses and went home to Missouri, I was thankful, not that he was gone, but that I had had the opportunity to bring something to a close and get on with my life. I felt relieved. I felt light. I felt free. Now I could have a relationship with a man unimpaired by the missing pieces of the past. And that is what I wanted. I figured I would not hear from Dick again, except through Shannon and Louise, if he chose to stay in contact.

Well, I started getting letters, lots of letters, letters suggesting he was still in love with me and maybe we could try it again. At first I laughed and threw the letters away, but as time went by, I began to write back. When Dick came up for horse shows, he would visit. He asked Barbara to move out. A part of me felt vindicated. It was only right that she should be on the other end of the stick . . . I didn't like feeling that way, but I told myself it was karmic.

That was the start of seven more years with Dick. Eventually he moved back to Minnesota. We did a lot of healing during that time. We made peace with the past through innumerable storms and upsets. He came to understand how hurt I had been. I learned that though the hurt kept surfacing, I had to let it go. I could tell him about my anger, my hurt, but I couldn't keep whipping it out and beating him with it. He couldn't change the past nor could I, we could only be with each other in the present as fully as we knew how, taking care of today.

Our daughter Shannon was in drug treatment while we were together the second time. During Family Week we learned that Dick's relationship to horses was like an addiction: It was his primary relationship, nurtured at the expense of everything else—wife, children, home, money. Once we both saw that, the heartache of our marriage was easier to put into perspective. Horses aren't your conventional drug. Dick used to say, "What are you complaining about? I'm working long hours, putting in all this time for our future. I'm not drinking or gambling." And I felt crazy because he wasn't drinking or gambling, and yet the horses had taken over so completely that they were a fix, not just a nice part of life, not just something that he could take or leave.

We were dealing with an addiction. We were dealing with an affair. We were dealing with my undeveloped sense of self, my codependency, and my lack of self-esteem. Having both done some thinking about our lives, we learned from those mistakes. The second chance was truly was a gift. Yet part of the gift after the healing was the opportunity for me to come to grips with our differences, something I didn't do the first time around. I know who Dick is, his essence, his core, and that is what I love. I couldn't reconcile that with his aloof silences.

We went through a lot of counseling. After several months, I noticed that I was coming into every single session with the same frustration—how to get a response. Every week we would go home and nothing changed, nothing opened up, nothing moved. Finally, I got so bored hearing myself say the same thing week in and week out that I decided I needed to take a new action, change the dance, if you will. So I forewarned Dick, "I am going to say things to you once, maybe twice, max. If you don't respond, I'll back off and do what I need to do to get whatever it is handled."

I knew this was the ultimate risk. He might come forward if I backed off; he might have a chance to bring something to the relationship he couldn't bring while I was wanting more. On the other hand, I might find out that silent is just how he is, no malice intended, no change likely in this lifetime. I was living in hope that the former was true. As long as I didn't test it, maybe . . . I dreaded seeing the reality of the latter.

The new dance gave me perspective. I saw what I didn't want to see, but it was clear and gave me something to go on. It was as if I had been playing tennis with myself, game after game, hitting the ball over the net and crashing over to the other court, forehand, backhand, smash, whatever—to keep that ball in play. A regular one-woman Wimbledon. No wonder I was tired. I had to ask myself, Why would anyone do that?

One evening at dinner, after I had been saying things only once, twice max, for about two weeks and then backing off, I asked Dick if he noticed the change. He looked up from his bratwurst. "It's really great, kind of peaceful," he smiled. For me though, it was lonely. Dick hadn't come forward more, he just continued on, quietly contented. It felt to me like there was no one there. We were two entities with very different needs, coexisting. At least when I was haranguing him, as uncomfortable as it was, we were engaged.

I began to give a lot of thought to ending the relationship. I'd met a man who represented another way of being a man—outgoing, warm, responsive, involved with his children. Although I didn't date him until some months later, watching him had expanded my world, sort of like traveling to a different city does, or vacationing in a milder climate. He reminded me that relationships needn't be so hard. I second-guessed myself: What if Dick is a diamond in the rough and I just don't get it, even after all this time? What if I'm making a huge mistake? What if I just tried a little harder? Maybe I'm just not accepting enough and I will regret this decision later. Maybe I'll be a lonely old woman, wishing I hadn't said good-bye.

But I felt older than I thought forty-two should feel, and too tired to go on. I wasn't ready to cash in my chips, to become resigned to such a lonely existence now. The many years I had been single taught me that life can be full with or without a relationship, and I was willing to risk being without one. I told Dick about the man I had met, that I was attracted to him, but I wasn't dating him, and that I was thinking of leaving. I wanted it all out on the table.

That week he suggested we go to a bed and breakfast in Wisconsin, something I had been asking him to do for five years. He even made the reservation. We had a wonderful time. He started listening to me and responding. His sympathy, when I was tired after a hard day, didn't turn me into a sniveling weenie like he had feared it would. Instead, I felt known, understood. He told me that I was a good horsewoman and that he liked working horses with me, something that, even after all those years we had ridden together, he had never said. It was like good air in a stuffy room. It was so right and so easy. I was deeply touched.

But it was too late. Ernie Larson, a popular speaker on relationships, says, "Guys, women have a very long rope. But when they start telling you they are at the end of it, they mean they are at the end of it. A lot of men are surprised when a woman leaves, even though she has been letting him know things weren't right for a long time. A lot of times, if the man is comfortable he thinks there's not a problem. Wake up. If she's making noises, she means it!" Timing is everything.

Once I let go of the relationship, I could let Dick be Dick. Funny, I started loving him again with an open heart. All the while we were trying to be partners with such different needs and expectations, he always felt that he was lacking, that he just couldn't make it with me. And he couldn't. I needed more interaction. That is all. Now that I'm not trying to get it from him, I can sincerely say, "Be blessed. You are a good man." And I picture his cute butt and bowlegs wrapped happily around the back of a horse, his blue eyes taking in the good land where he lives. Or I see him sitting outside the tack shed with three or four of his friends, old cowboys on a bench spinning yarns, and Dick mostly listening.

The other day Louise and I were out riding at the farm where I board my horse. She hadn't seen her dad in a long time. He doesn't call her, but when she calls him, he is always happy to hear from her. I said, "You know, when I think of Dick, I know him as a man of love and a man of deep connection to the earth. He is a big soul in a body that can't seem to reach out. I feel sad about that, but maybe it's not sad for him. I don't know. All I know is about wanting to love that man, wanting you and Shannon to be able to love him like I loved my dad, and feel his love in return."

I told her about George, an acquaintance who, for many, many years, couldn't express himself, either. His life as a traveling salesman gave him little opportunity to connect with his wife or children. Because he felt extremely awkward about showing his emotions, this was fine with him. But often, when the workday was over and night fell, he would lie in bed thinking, "I wish I could tell my son I love him." And he would fall asleep, anguished that he could not speak what was in his heart, knowing he would be on the road again in the morning.

I told Louise about big Tom, who, when we were cramped together in a small car on the way to a conference in Chicago, told me how he had been so inward, so unresponsive that his wife could take no more. "Leave," she told him, "or get help. I'm done." The asphalt clicked under the tires as he went on.

"I remember sitting on the edge of the bed, trying to get words out of my mouth. I couldn't move, I couldn't speak. I could only look down at my feet on the floor next to the bed. My wife thought I was a monster, but I just couldn't get hold of what was inside. I loved her, I loved my family. Nothing came out. I was shaking there on the bed, knowing I could lose it all, and I literally couldn't do anything about it."

Both of these men, on the brink of disaster or after the fact, did do personal work that has enabled them to break the silence and share their love openly. They are butterflies as surely as any, flying on wings that bring freedom, joy, intimacy, self-expression. Whatever chasm they had to cross, whatever abyss they faced, they have come back, each from his own journey and each still on it, lighting the way, telling what it is like to be in a skin called strong silent man. I never knew. I never knew. And Dick could not tell me.

I thank these men for being the shamans who bridge the worlds of the inner and outer, the male and the female, for forging the way for their brothers and healing the wounds that tear us apart.

I don't regret the decision I made. Leaving the relationship with Dick was a leap of faith, a listening to that inner knowing that said, "Go, there is no more to do here." Only then could I love Dick unconditionally. Only then could my anger turn into compassion, and my life be filled full again with people and things that fly on brightly colored wings.

A One-Woman Wimbledon

Finding Your Stories

1. Have you ever met someone who took you right back to another time in your life? Tell about that person, what you found out about yourself, where he or she took you.

2. Do you ever wonder how many times you meet someone and they don't really get to know you? For them, you represent their parent, an old lover, or maybe a teacher they didn't get along with. Tell a story about being with someone who related to you as though you were someone else.

3. Make up a story that completes a missing piece in your life.

4. Sometimes answers or insights come from unexpected places, not from the person we would like them from. What chance meetings, borrowed books, or stolen moments of doing nothing have helped you see something in a new way?

5. What life-altering decision have you made that you have never regretted? What led up to it? How did it change you? How did it affect others?

6. Tell about a second chance. Was it a rerun? A new beginning? A coming home? A going backward? A detour? A release?

Some People You Will Always Love

S o many old friends under the stars eating from paper
plates. A casual party, I expected it to be easy. I looked
forward to seeing people I hadn't seen in years at the
reunion I had helped plan.

After my divorce several years ago, I joined a group called
We Care. My sister-in-law, Jean, had heard about it from a
friend whose divorce had left her a mess, but when Jean saw
her friend a year later, she looked good, felt good, and loved

her life. "We Care," she told Jean. "It did me worlds of good."

Before I went to any meetings, a woman friend and I heard about a We Care-sponsored dance held in a loft over an antique store in South Minneapolis. We decided it would be a great way to spend a Saturday night, maybe even meet someone.

"What a group of losers!" I thought, after just one look around. A very tall, spindly man in cranberry polyester slouched around the edge of the dance floor, kinetic but too shy to rock and roll. A little while later the band struck up a confident "Hava Nagila." A five-foot brunette bundle of curves and vitality, spilling out of a red jumpsuit with a plunging neckline, led a circle of dancers. Faster and faster they went, having a high old time. I snorted an "I would never stoop so low" kind of snort. My friend and I mingled for a while, but concluded we had nothing in common with these characters. The men, we agreed, were particularly unattractive, not our type at all.

The divorce had left me devastated. All the dances in the world were not going to put my world back together, and I knew it. But Jean kindly suggested—again—that I go to a We Care meeting. I wasn't so sure, but I trusted her and I was encouraged by remembering how her friend turned out. So I went.

I expected the worst. What would I, a hapless but noble victim of an unfortunate divorce, perpetrated by a lout of an ex-husband, have in common with a bunch of worldly, jaded people who obviously could not keep their marriages together. Surely, I was the exception, not the rule. If it weren't for him . . .

I attended the informal We Care groups for several months, repairing my heart in the hurting group, then moving on to other topics relevant to being single again: relationships, single parenting, dating, loneliness, friendship, sex. The people there were the kindest, wisest, most courageous and authentic group of people I had ever met. They illuminated my divorce experience with insights and anecdotes from their lives. They listened with respect to my point of view, allowing me to listen to myself in new ways, to heal my pain, and to rebuild my future. Simply showing up at weekly meetings, listening to others and being listened to, helped me quit blaming my ex-husband for everything. With the help of a caring community, I took my life back into my own hands.

I met new women friends. After playing the role of good

wife and mother for years, it was great to have fun again with girlfriends. I hadn't realized how I had missed the support and camaraderie of other women. Linda and I had kids the same age. Shirley and I eventually bought a house together. Jane asked me why I didn't take a break from dating for a while and get to know myself in a new way. Judy and I went skiing in the Canadian Rockies over Easter break one year.

I met new men friends. I had never had men friends before. As a child, I attended Catholic schools where they separated the boys from the girls, so I never knew quite what species boys belonged to, nor did I know what to do in their presence. In We Care, men talked to women and to each other. They listened to women and to each other. It was enlightening to realize that men were real human beings. Bruce and I wrote poetry. Harold talked to me about dreams. Jim had parties. Carl got into cooking.

I began to date different men. I had married right out of high school, the second man I fell in love with. My first love, in eighth grade, jilted me for a summer romance with a girl from Iowa. If you count Gregory Anderson in fourth grade, then my husband would have been my third love. (I knew Gregory loved me because he threw my tennis shoes down the sewer during a great big storm.)

In any case, after my divorce, I made up for the dating I hadn't done in high school. I dated my karate instructor, a former tennis star, a truck driver, an engineer, and a financial planner. Eventually, I met a junior high school teacher named John Cook at one of the classes that We Care occasionally sponsored.

John was a stocky, bearded man. We hit it off at once, once we noticed each other, that is. It's funny how, if you give yourself time to know people, they get better. I wouldn't have been attracted to John had I not gotten to know him over the weeks in class.

We went dancing. We read poems to each other. We wrote our own. We camped. We cuddled. I told him about that first We Care dance and how everyone there looked like a loser.

"I was there," John said.

Our relationship grew. I loved John dearly. I said to him, "I want a commitment."

In truth, I was pretty ambivalent about another marriage and the four children we would have between us—his two boys and my two girls. The thought of daily household chores and keeping track of schedules throttled the romance right out of me. I would become what I was before, I just knew it—a non-person in charge of other people's messes. I had become pretty cynical.

John said, "I am not ready for a commitment." He said it regretfully but with conviction.

Neither one of us was completely honest. I should have said, "I am not ready for a commitment, as much as the idea appeals to me." He should have said, "I do not want to be committed to you." That fall, John married Ginger, a woman who taught at the same junior high school he did.

The We Care Reunion was held in Barbara Witte's sprawling suburban backyard. Potluck. BYOB. A familiar way to play. Everyone we could find since We Care began was invited, including John. Although he did not RSVP, I had heard that he might be there.

The talk was easy as people piled out of cars and wandered across Barbara's thick lawn, clustering into little knots under the trees. I hoped I looked good.

More people arrived. Many I knew, some I didn't. Over on the patio, a lawyer I had never met was expounding on his last trip to Italy. A few people gathered around, fascinated by his tales. Others drifted away across the cool grass to friends sitting on blankets scattered on the ground.

On my way into the house for more ice, the strangest thing happened. It was as if time and space were suspended. I noticed the design of the plastic forks on their way into open mouths, the exquisite scalloped edges of the paper plates. I noticed the brown screen door as it contrasted with the textured beige Masonite siding and how a fly hovered motionless, droning over the porch light.

It had been five years since I danced ever so slowly with John, laid my head against his beard, and he was standing beside me now on the porch.

Inside I could hear people sucking olives off toothpicks. I could hear ice dropping into glasses, and laughter, thin as the crackling ice and far away. My breath tore outside for air.

Like a dreaming dog's foot, John's smile twitched through "Hello, Lynn." His wife, Ginger, stood by his side, polite. I stood there, too, chatting above the din of my heart, wondering what to do with my arms, which foot to shift my weight to next.

All night the two of us watched each other not watch each other. When we were dating, John liked to circulate at parties, to not be too much of a couple. "Maintain your identity as individuals," he would always say. At this party he and

Ginger were as tight as a hand in a glove.

The wine I had brought was making me sleepy. I drank it anyway. Out on the patio, three couples danced to Neil Diamond and the purple rhythm of the bug zapper. Around midnight, in the kitchen, a short drunk man nuzzled an even shorter disheveled woman. Soon after I walked in on them, they left the party. I leaned against the Formica counter to reflect on this. When I looked up, John's blue eyes were dancing with me. We were alone together for one brief moment.

"I think about you . . . often . . ." he whispered.

Something moved in me, naturally as rain drawn up and out through the stem of a willow. Some people you will always love, even though the time was not right for more, even though you have filled your life full again and made peace with their absence. Sometimes you wonder if you are loved like that, too.

I touched John's cheek with my finger and brushed it lightly across his lips. Slowly he turned to go home.

I have kept his gift.

Some People You Will Always Love

Finding Your Stories

1. Tell a story about a party.

2. Tell about a moment that was very, very right.

3. Tell about a first impression.

4. Tell about getting to know someone or something that you didn't like at first.

5. Tell about a time when words were unnecessary.

6. Tell about someone you will always love.

Being with Gary 20 or 30 More Times

or . . .

Looking for Prince Charming in the Twilight Zone

Harold was driving me out to Shirley's house in Minnetonka for one of her famously fun dinner parties. All single again, the women and men in our little group had developed a nice camaraderie as we played together and grieved together, laughed, cried, wrote poems, danced, and listened to one another after our divorces. We built new lives as single people with each other's kind, though sometimes quirky, support.

Harold, I'd say, was one of the quirkiest. Fat and bald, an accountant by trade, he wore suits most of the time. He drove a big white Buick, substantial enough to bulldoze a stand of mature oaks. He refused to ride in my little orange Volkswagen bug because, to his way of thinking, a car symbolizes your life journey, and he could not career through life or even to Minnetonka in a vehicle as flimsy as mine.

Dreams were important to Harold. He could be sitting at a Chinese New Year's banquet table with ten perfect strangers and have the man across from him discussing the possibility that they had met before on the astral plane. He thought a lot about past lives. He carried index cards in his shirt pocket on which to write words or phrases that resonated with whatever soulful thing he was inquiring into at the time. He spent one whole winter fixing old television sets so he could learn about opening up new channels in his life. Before he spoke, he always took a deep breath.

On the way out to Shirley's, I told Harold about my breakup with Gary, with whom I had fallen madly in love, but who thought I wanted too much sex and said that commitment wouldn't work for him at all, especially if we had to talk about it. Harold listened and listened as I told my sad, sad story.

"What do you think, Harold?" I asked when I had shared all the painful details.

Harold took a deep breath. "What did you learn from being with Gary?" he asked me back. I replied, "I learned, once again, that you can't trust men. I learned that men don't want commitment. I learned that Gary is scum. I learned that dating is only for masochists. I learned that . . ." We were almost to Shirley's.

"Oh," said Harold, taking another deep breath. "Then you can count on going through this same thing twenty or thirty more times."

"What do you mean by that!" I snapped. I wanted sympathy, not threats. "There's no way I'm going to go through this again, and besides, what do you know about my future?"

We pulled into Shirley's driveway. Harold liked drama as much as I did. This was his moment to look at me significantly and say nothing.

We had a fabulous time at Shirley's. She was one of the few people I knew who still enjoyed the pleasure of setting a beautiful table. That night the dishes were a bright red, yellow, and blue farmyard motif. The wine was cheap but tasty. The talk was grand.

After dinner we gathered in the living room to visit and sip wine around a great crackling fire. The topic turned to relationships, and of course I had to retell the whole tragic story of my breakup with Gary. The people there were much more sympathetic than Harold had been, offering me words of comfort and assurance. I liked that. Harold had not said anything for a long time. He took a deep breath. "So who did you learn about in this relationship?" he inquired from his seat deep in the cushions of the overstuffed sofa. He paused significantly. The room was quiet.

"Oh." I went over the whole thing again in my mind, like a tape on very fast forward. "OH . . . I guess I learned about myself." That put the relationship in a whole new light.

I had never told Gary I was interested in commitment. I didn't want to scare him. I had never told him I was ambivalent about it, too. I didn't want to seem scatter-brained. I never asked Gary what he wanted. I never asked him about sexuality. I assumed all men enjoyed a certain amount of sex. There were a lot of things that I didn't express in order to hedge my bets for the kind of outcome I wanted. I didn't see all of this until Harold asked me who I learned about as a result of being with Gary, but yeah, I learned a lot about me.

"Well, now you'll only have to go through this kind of thing one, maybe two more times. Just a little more practice and you're home free." And Harold went back to sipping his wine.

Being with Gary 20 or 30 More Times

Finding Your Stories

1. We all have secret mentors. They often ask us the hard questions. Which people ask you questions that make you think about old habits in new ways? Have you ever thanked them? If not, do it today. If yes, thank them again.

2. Can you think of people you wouldn't ordinarily listen to who might have something to contribute to you? How would you have to listen to get value from what they say?

3. If there's a pattern in your life that you complain about, look again. Do you blame your dissatisfaction on what is "out there," like I did? I really believed that men don't commit, that you can't trust them, and that I knew how to have a relationship and they didn't. It was those darn men. When the same kinds of men kept coming into my life, I had more validation for the way I saw things.

With Harold's hard question, I began to look at how much I didn't say or do, and how I was being as a partner.

- What lesson do you keep having to relearn?
- Can you rarely get a second date?
- Does no one listen to you?
- Do you get a new job and wind up hating your employer?
- What do you say to yourself when you find yourself in a similar situation over and over?
- Whom do you learn about?

4. Find some humor in one of your recurring lessons. What is the joke?

5. Make up a fairy tale with you as the unfortunate heroine (or hero). Put her (or him) through at least as many trials as you have had. Make up more. What does she do? How does she come through it all? Make up several different endings.

6. Have you been to any memorable dinner parties? Who was there? Was there a character there or a topic of conversation that you particularly remember? Was there a moment when things shifted, came together, or fell apart? Where does this memory take you?

7. A car provides its own little world. Tell about a car ride, going somewhere or coming home, by yourself or with others.

The Personals and Mr. Right

I placed my first personal ad a few months after parting with Carl, a summer love. I had spent the fall and winter staring at the walls of my bedroom. One early spring day, I was done moping. I needed to do something.

On a sunny morning after breakfast, I was absentmindedly paging through one of the old *Twin Cities Readers* that littered my butcher block counter. I was first amused by, then suddenly intrigued by, the possibility of the personal ads that filled the back pages of the paper. Right then and there I decided to place a personal ad of my own.

I looked at the ads again. What did people say? Where should I begin? Every ad I looked at went something like this:

"Prince Charming wishes to meet Cinderella."

It seemed that everyone who placed an ad was fit, attractive, flawless. They were looking for same. I was completely intimidated. Surely that was not me.

So this is the ad I ran:

"Plain old regular ordinary human being type female seeks plain old regular ordinary human being type male for dynamite relationship." I included my height so short men would not be surprised by a 5'9" woman. I mentioned the fact that I had two children, so no one at all would be surprised. I specified nonsmoker.

Because I had misgivings about what kind of people placed personal ads, I didn't tell a soul about my little adventure. Even though the ad might read "fit, attractive, and flawless," I still read "desperate, kinky, and sleazy." Certainly I wasn't sleazy.

These days when you place an ad, you can receive your responses by mail, or you can choose a voicemail option. Back then, in the early eighties, you had to go downtown to the *Reader* office and pick up your mail. It took about two weeks from the day you placed your ad to the time you could pick up your responses, so if you were desperate to begin with, the wait cooled you down. On the fourteenth day, I hopped into my orange Volkswagen bug and headed downtown.

I found a parking place right in front of the building that housed the *Reader* offices. Although it was highly unlikely that anyone noticed or cared that I had placed an ad for a date, I slid quickly out of my car into the building, sneaked past the candy and cigarette lady in the lobby, and stepped nonchalantly into the waiting elevator. Nuts. There was a man in the elevator getting off on the fourth floor too. I waited until I was sure he was headed down a different hall-way, and tiptoed past closed office doors until I found the *Reader* office. The door was open. I swallowed hard and walked in.

"Hi. I'm Lynn Baskfield," I mumbled, looking at my shoe. "I'm ad number 2601. I came to pick up my responses."

"Oh, 2601," the woman at the desk shouted. "The mail slots are right in there." She made a sweeping gesture with her arm. "You have a ton of mail."

I swallowed. I walked into the mail room. My box was overflowing with envelopes of all shapes and sizes. I had visualized not getting any responses and going home rejected by a city full of men I didn't even know. The only thing worse than getting no mail was to get so much I had to use two arms to carry it. Now everyone would know for sure that I was reduced to this to get a date.

But I was fascinated. Could it be? As soon as I got to the car, I counted the envelopes. Thirty-five. What was I going to do with thirty-five men? One fat letter addressed in calligraphy caught my attention. I opened it then and there. Inside were eight pages of musings from a rather interesting-sounding man.

As soon as I got home, I plopped down on the couch and tore into the rest of my mail. This was beginning to be fun. I separated everything into piles—Yes, No, and Maybe. Then I called my friend Nancy.

"Guess what I did! I placed a personal ad a couple of weeks ago, and I've got thirty-five letters right here. You've got to come over and look at them." Nancy came right over.

We were like little kids.

"I like this one."

"Take that out of Maybes and put it in with the Yeses."

"This is definitely a No."

"It is not. It's not your ad. I'm keeping it a Yes."

We giggled and we argued. Then Nancy said, "So when are you going to call these people?"

My stomach gripped. Now that I'd done this, I supposed I should follow through. Help.

I called Mr. Calligraphy. We had one date. He was a nice enough sort, very intense and slightly depressed. Our conversation was endlessly significant. I wanted a little more lightness.

I also went out with a young, blond fledgling guitar player who worked for the railroad. I liked him. We set up another date, which he canceled the day we were to go out because some guys he knew wanted him to go to a guy thing with them instead. He was sincerely apologetic and proposed that we reschedule, but anyone who has children knows that getting out of the house requires the combined skills of a choreographer, a long-distance runner, and a strategic planner. Rescheduling on such short notice didn't work for me. We never spoke again.

The truth was, I was gratified to know that there were so many decent-sounding men out there. But I didn't know what to do with them now that they were within my reach. I felt like a state fair jelly judge. A little tart. Too sweet. Needs clarity.

Even throwing out all the No's, I couldn't see how to work the logistics of dating twenty men, and, God knows, at that time it was difficult for me to tell the truth if I thought it would hurt someone's feelings. It didn't occur to me that when people answer an ad, they know there will be others in the running. Any given meeting may or may not be a fit. No big deal. Let's just have fun. See what we see. Maybe make a new friend.

Needless to say, if Mr. Right was in that batch of mail, he remained just a letter and a name. My balloon lost its lift before I could get to him.

A couple of years later, I placed another ad. I'd been doing some thinking. *Partnership* was a word that fascinated me. Women and men learning to be partners. So I said I was looking for "a bright, caring man willing to create a nurturing partnership with a spiritual dimension." I again listed my height and number of children and specified a nonsmoker.

I was not afraid this time. I undertook the process of meeting people with enthusiasm. There were not nearly so many letters this time. Being more specific narrows things down. But, even so, people read a lot into things.

For instance, a phone conversation with one man who wrote a good letter turned out to be very weird. He had picked up on the spiritual part. It seems he had started his own church and sometime soon he wanted me to come up to his apartment and see his religious artifacts. I should have known then to decline a dinner invitation. But I still suffered from chronic niceness. I placed the ad; I must owe him an evening. So we met at The Black Forest Inn.

He was extremely intense. "Am I a magnet for intense men?" I asked myself. His face was gaunt. He chain smoked. He looked like Charles Manson, the 1960s cult leader from California. Over dinner he again invited me to his apartment to see his religious artifacts. This I declined. Enough of being nice. I had my limits. I reminded him that the ad said nonsmoker. "You must try to be less rigid," he intoned.

I met several other people, and although they were fine human beings, we didn't click. I was to meet one more fellow for lunch at Winfield Potter's, an upscale restaurant overlooking the Mississippi River. His name was Rich. As we chatted our way through the buffet line, I secretly thought, "No way." His business suit hung on his rail-thin frame. Fine, dishwater blond hair fell into his eyes, and he wore a mustache that scraggled down over his upper lip. I wanted to trim it right then and there. He had a funny, New Jersey accent.

We talked more over lunch. He was bright but not a bit

arrogant. He had an easy way about him. The conversation was polite, but I was thinking in subtitles. Out loud I said, "What kind of computers do you work with?" To myself I said, "How can he eat with his mustache in his mouth?" Out loud, "Tell me about why you answered my ad." To myself, "How could anyone make love to someone that skinny?" It was like a scene from the old Woody Allen movie *Annie Hall*.

It was a fine lunch. He was a fine person. I noticed that he could eat just fine with his scraggly mustache. I was glad to go home. I didn't plan to call him nor did I expect to hear from him again. That week he called. He wanted to go out again. I wasn't so hot on the idea, but he wasn't pushy, and he included my kids in the invitation. I was planning on taking them to the State Fair anyway, so I said yes. We had a great time.

Rich kept calling, but not pushing. I grew fond of his New Jersey accent. We started dating. Eventually I trimmed his mustache. We enjoyed the things they always list in the personals—long walks, fine wine, good music. We canoed out to his island cabin near the Boundary Waters and spent long weekends. Indeed, he was skinny, but he was bright, lively, caring, and he didn't smoke. We got along quite well. But in the end, we wanted different things out of life. A year and a half later, though we remained friends, we went our separate ways.

So I did not meet Mr. Right then, either.

These ads have been like a public notice of my evolution regarding relationships. Over the next few years, I thought a lot about what I really wanted. All along, since my divorce in the midseventies, I thought I wanted a committed relationship. It looked to me that men, as a group, did not want to be committed. At least that was my experience. My husband had left. The men I dated, after some time went by and we grew closer, would shrivel up and die at the mention of possible commitment.

As I looked harder at commitment as a question, not as an answer, things began to change. I saw that indeed there were men who were committed—just not to me. And that I was the one who was scared to death of commitment. *Moi?* The finger pointed this way. Now what?

I saw that I didn't want to scare anyone off by saying clearly at the outset that I was really looking for commitment. So of course, I attracted people who didn't know about my desire for a lasting relationship until later in the game. Surprise! We had signed up for different programs.

I saw that although I said I wanted commitment, if someone had actually shown up at my doorstep who was ready to be my partner, I would have run the other way. I saw that, to me, commitment meant obligation. It meant not being myself. It meant giving up the things I love for someone else. It meant having children together, then raising the kids alone.

I couldn't get a grip on what commitment is, so by default, I began to get some idea of what it isn't. I saw that it isn't obligation, that obligation is deadening. Not a lot of joy exists in it.

Commitment is alive, empowering, enriching. It doesn't imprison you or tie you down. It gives you freedom to create something you see as possible. It gives you a framework on which to build.

So more years went by. I dated a few people during that time and even did some healing with my ex-husband. By the time I put my last ad in, I ran this headline:

Love and Freedom Are Not Opposites

I started right out with "Fit, outdoorsy, vital woman 5'9", looking for committed partnership with bright, independent, loving man."

Oh, the swashbuckling replies. I met men I would never have met any other way and found myself in places I would never have gone had I not been invited by these dear souls. By this time I was not afraid at all. Placing an ad was like an exploration for me. Even though a man might not strike me as Mr. Right, I could still enjoy what he was about in his life and share mine with him. I could let these men contribute something of themselves to me.

One man was a former CIA agent and undercover drug runner in the Florida Keys during the elder President Bush's War on Drugs. He was a combination good Catholic boy and devil-may-care adventurer. I could not see myself with someone who lives a secret life, but I was struck by his love for justice and his direct action in an area that concerned him deeply.

He was also in the military. Our first meeting took place at the Officers Club. I sat waiting for him at a table near the glowing fireplace. The orange flames jumped and flickered. As I picked up my wine, I noticed the bullet design on the tabletop—real bullet casings embedded in a circular motif under Plexiglas.

He arrived a few minutes later. Even though he was in the military, he was against war. Interesting. A visionary of sorts.

A man with much courage who felt he could make a difference from within and was willing to take an unpopular position.

I met a very handsome, intense musician. Yes, I get at least one intense one per ad. Over our first dinner, he brought the conversation right around to the subject of death. It was taking him quite a long time to recover from the death of his father and, as the conversation wore on, from his father's life as well. His father had many, many faults. We saw each other a few more times, but in my opinion, he liked brooding about recovering from things rather than actually recovering, and that didn't work for me.

I met a delightful science professor who prided himself on being from New York. He described himself as outlandishly aggressive with a heart of mush. We became friends. He couldn't see being in a romantic relationship with a woman who was raised Catholic, though, because he was Jewish, and he felt strongly that all Catholics blame all Jews for killing Christ. This seemed pretty far out to me. My spiritual path was one of inquiry and exploration, not one of dogma and blame, and I had never met someone who made such categorical pronouncements before. But anti-Semitism was a very personal thing for him, and even though we had many lively discussions about spiritual things, he could never really trust my views.

Marty was a tossed salad. In certain areas, he had all the answers. He knew how life was, and he would not look at what might be possible. On the other hand, he had a curiosity that led him beyond himself, but only where it was safe, like in science or in having harmless fun. For instance, one of his students invited him to the Ogilvie Traffic Watch. He asked me to go along. It was one of my more memorable dates.

· Every year on the Friday evening before the opening of fishing season, an Ogilvie, Minnesota, hog farmer, whose farm is situated right on State Highway 65, a main road north, hosts the Traffic Watch. This was the twelfth annual event. Traffic watchers come from far and wide to have some fun with the steady stream of cars passing by, their drivers and passengers dreaming of the lunkers they'll land at Mille Lacs or Big Sandy or lakes beyond. Signs like old Burma Shave ads warn travelers of the gauntlet they will soon pass through.

> *Honk your horn*
> *Strike up the band*
> *The traffic watch is coming up*
> *Ain't it lovely, ain't it grand*

Then, as cars snake bumper to bumper up the highway, traffic watchers sit by the side of the road, rating each car with numbered signs just like in the Olympics. The numbering system at the Traffic Watch goes from +10 to −10. Drivers and passengers give it their best, honking, calling, waving. Each year you can count on getting mooned at least once. Mooners usually get a solid 10.

A potluck, brats on the grill, and a live rock and roll band add to the festivities. Marty and I got a tour of the hog barns. We had taken my car, but I asked Marty to drive home. New Yorkers, I began to realize during the ride, don't drive much. We lurched home through detours and over unfamiliar gravel roads. Marty was trying to be gracious, but he was white as a sheet by the time we grazed the curb in front of my house. He got on his trusty ten-speed, which he had locked to my lamppost, and pedaled home.

Very shortly after that, Marty met a Jewish woman who fit all his criteria, and he moved in with her.

I did not meet Mr. Right through that ad either. But I have met him. We are not very much alike.

I met Bill at my daughter's high school graduation party where we were both volunteers. I was wearing my daughter's fake fur, zip-up, South High tiger mascot suit with eyebrow pencil whiskers drawn across my cheeks. Some time later, Bill confided that at first he didn't find me especially attractive. (Gee, I thought the suit was pretty alluring, especially with the whiskers.) But as we got to know each other, he said, "Finding you was like finding a beautiful shell on the beach when I wasn't even looking." I thought, "Wow, is he for real?"

He was for real. We were friends for a long time before we were lovers. We have been together now for more than ten years. We would never have answered each other's personal ads because we approach life in different ways and use different words for things. For instance, he would not have responded to anything with the word *spiritual* in it, although he is a spirited, soulful man. Nor would he have particularly resonated with the terms *outdoorsy* or *vegetarian*. Although he appreciates the beauty of city and country, he is a businessman, not an outdoorsman, and he could eat a good hamburger every day of the week. To him, tofu is a joke.

I would not have responded to an ad saying "father of small boy." My daughters are grown now, and I had considered child rearing a thing of the past. Nor would I have answered an ad that mentioned a love for long-distance bicycling. I ride my horse once a week. I ride my bike two or three times a year—and that's in a good year.

But something is there for us that cannot be captured in matching words or in opinions that ride the same rail. It is an authenticity that is the essence of intimacy. It is a commitment to creating a partnership that nurtures both of us, and even though neither of us has any particular idea of how to do that, we roll up our sleeves and do it every day. We laugh. We play. We talk to each other. We make good love. We bring out the creativity in one another. We keep each other honest.

Being together, we see that truly, love and freedom are not opposites.

The Personals and Mr. Right

Finding Your Stories

1. Have you ever done something impulsive? Not like you at all? What happened?

2. Write a personal ad. Don't give it too much thought, just dash it off. Now write another one. Now another one. How many sides of you are there? How different or the same does each ad sound? Have fun with this.

3. Write a personal ad being someone else. "Looking for romance. Church lady seeks Wednesday night date for vesper services, Friday choir practice, and Sunday horse shoe tournaments. Must be able to lambada. Pets okay, especially fond of iguanas." Write another and another. Who are these characters, anyway?

4. Think of ten things that you would like to acquire or get rid of. Make your declaration to the universe in a classified ad format. Positions Wanted. For Sale. Home Services. Health. Room for Rent. Auditions. . . . You make it up!

5. Tell about a character you dated.

6. Tell about a date from hell.

7. Play with some stories about relationships. Tell the same story from a number of vantage points: yours, the dog's, a fly on the wall, your mother's, your friend's, your fairy godmother's.

The Man with No Trunks Who Liked to Be Right

Y ou can't miss my six-foot-seven-inch friend John. I met him through a personal ad. When I walked into Pasqual's Salsaria on a rainy summer evening to meet him for tacos, I knew right away that he was completely wrong for me. He was ten years younger, talked at length about bicycles, and all I wanted to do was go home. But somewhere between the last nacho and dessert, the conversation shifted. We talked about our work and satisfaction and being involved in something bigger than ourselves and how one creates that. I heard myself agreeing to spend another evening with him, but that would be it. Much to my surprise, a friendship grew and that is what it is today. John is a good friend, a brilliant listener, and someone who inspires me to be my best self.

Sometimes John and I tell stories on ourselves to let the other remind us again of who we really are and what we're really up to—given the idiosyncrasies that are part of each one of us.

For instance, I am abominably nice all the time, at the expense of being clear and truthful. Nice can be a good thing, but it can also be the thing that keeps me from expressing myself fully. Nice is like a voice that only sings middle C: It doesn't have much range.

I will call John and tell him about letting a salon customer cancel at the last minute without enforcing my twenty-four-hour cancellation policy. How can I ask someone to pay for an unkept appointment, even if it leaves me unable to fill it again on such short notice? John will remind me to look at what I'm committed to—integrity and well-being, yes? Being firm does not mean I'm a mean person. Taking care of my well-being and keeping myself and my clients observant of our integrity is really what I'm about, he'll remind me.

And, he says, "you will always start with your software defaulted on the 'nice' program. It just doesn't have to run the show." I thank him, hang up, and am able to say what I have to say to my client.

John, on the other hand, likes to get things right. He tries to figure things out to the nth degree so they are neatly packaged in rational, logical, easily reconstructed, unalterable boxes. The other day he called to talk to me about this requirement that he get things right at the expense of just being okay with things as they are.

John drives a school bus. When he was learning to drive a bus, he was all atwitter about whether or not he would ever get all the rules and regulations right, all the procedures and policies. I told him to just let himself learn, be willing to make mistakes, and not know for a time. He did that and became one of the best drivers in the fleet.

He told me that he's been noticing how unrelenting this getting-things-right business is, now that he's aware of it. It is everywhere. He hates it, now that he knows how to drive a bus right, when other bus drivers do things wrong. It's even worse with the average car driver on the street. What a bunch of bozos.

He says that he cleans the bus after a run because it is the right thing to do and there is a certain way to do it. One day, in an attempt to derail his automatic get-it-right reflex, he decided to clean the bus, not because it was right, but as a gift to the next driver. "But," he said, "I don't like giving anonymous gifts, so I don't think I've got it right yet."

"John, did you hear what you just said?" I asked.

He laughed. "I can't get away from it. Getting it right follows me, even when I'm trying not to try so hard to get it right."

"Yeah. Now you're trying to find a right way to change wanting to get things right. John, maybe you just need to accept that you like to get things right. That life for you is a struggle to get things right. With that in mind, maybe there can be a little lightness about it. It ain't going to go away. It's how you're wired up."

He laughed. "Aayyy!" he said. "I have to tell you a story about being right that really backfired on me. At the time I was mortified, but I can laugh about it now.

"Two years ago, I went cross country-skiing up in northern Minnesota with a group of friends. After a full day of skiing and a delicious home-cooked dinner, we fired up the sauna. The night was crisp and clear and, boy, was I was ready for the heat! But I wasn't quite sure if people were planning to go in with their bathing suits on or without. I didn't want to ask and look like a fool, but I didn't want to be out of sync with the crowd either, and look like a fool. I decided my best bet was to ask. I was told, 'No suits,' so I went in happily naked with everyone else.

"Well, last year the same group went skiing again. It was just great again, being out all day in that gorgeous country. After supper we fired up the sauna, and of course I knew the right thing to do—strip down to the skin and steam. I read for a little while after supper, so I was one of the last ones in the sauna that evening. I strode in, naked as a jaybird, only to discover that everyone else had suits on."

"What did you do?" I hooted, picturing his dilemma.

"I just sat down on the nearest bench and tried to be inconspicuous."

A naked six-foot-seven-inch man is hardly inconspicuous. I figured with everyone sitting on sauna benches, when John ducked through that little cedar door, his most interesting parts had to be right at eye level.

"After I sat down, the room went completely silent," he said. "I never felt less right than at that moment and the silence seemed endless. No one knew where to look. Suddenly one of the men ran outside to roll in the snow.

When he came back, he had left his bathing suit in the changing room. Others followed and pretty soon, the whole group, men and women alike, sat naked with me in the heat.

"Later that night, one of the guys thanked me for daring to take off my clothes. He had wanted to sauna naked too, and so had everyone else, but for some reason, no one had suggested it."

"You became a leader," I said. "You were just doing you, wanting to do it right, and everyone else saw you as daring and uninhibited."

We laughed. "Yeah," said John. "I guess it won't go away. It's just part of me. The sauna incident could have gone the other way too, with me slinking back to the changing room to find my trunks, but the good part is, I can at least see that being right is just part of being John. I can have fun with it, kind of ride it like a wave."

I smiled into the phone, not saying anything.

"Right?" he said.

The Man with No Trunks
Who Liked to Be Right

Finding Your Stories

1. Natalie Goldberg, an extraordinary writer *(Writing Down the Bones, Long Quiet Highway)* and a gifted teacher, says that to write anything at all, you have to be willing to write the worst shit in America. In other words, it's not always going to be right, but to get the flow going, to reach your deepest heart, your most authentic self, you have to be willing to just do it, and do it some more. Keep telling your stories. Listen to other people's stories. Trust the river. You will find your true stories by diving in. Go ahead. Write or tell a bad story.

2. Tell a story, do a dance, write a poem, make love. Do it right. Edit. Second-guess yourself. Check over your shoulder to see if you are being correct. Are you having fun yet? Are you present and accounted for? What is in the way?

3. Tell a story, do a dance, write a poem, make love. Forget the instructions, even these. Let go. Just do it. Move without looking back. Go from moment to moment, letting one word, idea, or movement reveal the next. Are you having fun yet? Letting go can be scary. Try it.

I Speak from the Wisdom of the Dark, Moist Places

I had never done a sweat lodge before. I had taken saunas but that wasn't the same, except the part where you sit in a small space, pour water over hot rocks, and sweat. Now, after a late April snow, I was sitting naked in a sweat lodge high in the Colorado Rockies with twelve other women.

You sit in a sauna only as long as you can take the heat. Then you run outside and plunge into a lake or a snowbank, depending on the season. When you are ready, you go back in again.

A sweat, on the other hand, takes as long as it takes.

The lodge is a small dome made of bent willows, symbolic of love that bends without breaking. Blankets and tarps cover the lodge so that once inside, no light enters. It doesn't matter if you have your eyes open or closed. It is so dark you can't even see the person sitting next to you. There are rounds where you sit in the lodge pouring water over white-hot rocks piled in a pit in the middle. The door flap is opened only between rounds for a few minutes to bring in air and more hot rocks. Then, intense heat again.

I was afraid I'd make a fool of myself having to crawl out into the cold air before everyone else because I couldn't stand the heat. Or maybe I would silently smother in there in the dark.

But the moment a small group of us began to assemble the volcanic rock in the late afternoon light, I knew I was a part of something sacred. I was surprised at the tears in my eyes and the choke in my voice as we dedicated each rock. "I ask that this rock represent the spirit of the horse." "I ask that this rock represent sight, both inner and outer." "I dedicate this rock to love and partnership." "I ask that this rock represent my mother and all the elders." We took turns until the many rocks were placed in a broad, shallow hole we had dug several feet away from the lodge. We listened to the wind in the pines. We welcomed the hoot of an owl. We built a huge pyramid of kindling and logs over the rocks and lit a fire that would burn for hours until the rocks held the fire within them. We thanked the wood and the rocks and the fire and the wind.

As night fell, more women arrived. Some were like me. This was their first sweat. Others had done sweats before. We sat in a circle around the blazing fire and talked about the lodge.

"The purpose of the sweat is to purify body, mind, and spirit," said Virginia, our leader. "At first only men did sweats. It was understood that women's monthly blood was a natural purification that returned power to the earth through the release of rich, fertile bodily fluids. Without this monthly renewal, the tribes believed they would not survive and the dreams of the people would die. Sweats were a way for men to give back to the earth with their bodies as well. Now, both men and women do sweats, but women don't need to do them as hot." She paused as we thought about this.

"Going into the sweat lodge is like going into the womb," she continued. "It is a place of renewal and rebirth."

She asked us to stand and speak our names and to call in

spirits of the seven directions. Then we sat again in silence as we prepared to enter.

The door flap was so low that to enter we had to kneel. Kneeling on the earth, Virginia explained earlier, was a reminder to remain humble. As we passed through the door we chanted, "ALL MY RELATIONS," to call to mind that others have gone before and that others will follow in an unbroken circle. We circled around the stone pit to the right, settled into the darkness, and after the woman who volunteered to be the stone carrier slid hot rocks into the lodge with a shovel, we closed the flap behind us.

Time dropped away and there was only now.

The ground is cold under my butt even though we are sitting on blankets. It is April and little signs of spring are all around, but the ground outside is still covered with snow. We offer tobacco to the rocks, then white sage. The burning sage makes the air smell pungent and clean. The hiss of water pouring over the rocks breaks the silence.

I'm not sure what to expect. Do we talk? Remain quiet? The steam wallops my lungs. I remember to breathe, not fight. The breathing brings me deeper. There is no place to go. Only my body, my lungs here in this darkness, which seems to be nowhere yet somehow central to all that exists. This darkness, this heat swallows me.

Deeper now, I see before me my mother's wrinkled face framed by soft gray hair.

I think about how I took this trip to sort out what has been happening. For a long time now, Mom has been slipping. Notes she writes to herself fail to jog her memory. She forgets when she is going to the doctor. She forgets that taxes aren't due every Friday. She has become frail and childlike, this once fiercely independent woman who carried chairs and beds from room to room if no one happened to be around when she got the itch to rearrange. When I was little, she held my hand crossing streets because I didn't look. Now we take walks again, and I hold her hand because she can't see.

In the vast darkness of the tiny lodge, I recall standing in a circle in the snow with the women here before we crawled into the sweat lodge. When we spoke our names they were not our regular first and last names, but our mothers' and grandmothers' names, the names of our daughters and our granddaughters, if we we had any. "I am Lynn, daughter of Dorothy, granddaughter of Emma and Louise, mother of

Louise and Shannon, grandmother of Jackae and Charmaine." I am touched by the imprint of the women's voices still with me, speaking into existence a missing strand of the web of life.

We know ourselves as the daughters of the fathers, the wives of the men. We don't often name ourselves as central in the long line of women. It is unfamiliar, affirming. I remember standing there in that circle, thinking men should have the opportunity to do this, too. It's like looking across from another hill. The view is much different. I think of the woman among us in the lodge who knows her grandmother was Indian, but has no record of her name. I wonder what happens to us when we forget our names and the stories that go with them.

I hear again how we invoked the seven directions as we prepared to enter the lodge: the North, South, East, West, the Above and Below, and the Center, or the Heart. In Native American culture, the heart is central. Things die without heart.

A drumbeat becomes a heartbeat in the darkness. A woman sighs into the heat, "I have loved long and well and now my love is gone." She cries, "I am so alone. I am so, so all alone." Softly, another voice responds, "I hear you."

Another and another. "I hear you. I hear you." Soon a chant-like cadenza of voices: "I hear you. You are heard. We are with you. What you feel is real. You are not alone, not alone, not alone. Speak and we will hear."

What would it be like, I wonder, if we could hear the heartbeat of our mothers' and grandmothers' lives? What if our lives and the lives of our daughters and granddaughters were given their authentic voice? What would it have been like if there was a place for women to go to honor their lives, their wombs, their pain, their passion, their knowing?

Now in the darkness in front of me I see the face of an enormous brown bear. The presence stays near me until the sweat is almost over. I feel its power and I feel strangely comforted. I am not at all frightened.

Later that night after the sweat was over, I found out that bear medicine is intuitive feminine knowing, going into the cave and coming out again, exactly the thing we were doing in the lodge.

It is in the coming out that we find our voices. We speak of what we have seen in the dark. Our words make the dark things light.

I saw so many things in the dark. I saw my mother, frail little Dorothy, walking the passage from the Good Red Road of Life to the Blue Road of Spirit. She was just walking down the road away from me, all by herself. Her step was slow but sure. I knew then that even though she was bargaining with life, she was really on her way over to the other side, and that she was okay. I saw that she needed to be on her way, with the love of family and friends her invisible companion.

My father died when I was fourteen. Soon after, Mom sold our house and we moved into an apartment. Mom went to appointments, played bridge, and took care of me as before. She didn't want to burden anyone with her sorrow, so she pretended not to grieve. I was the only child at home. I went back to ninth grade and acted like I did when I had a father. I didn't know how to express my grief, either. Even at home I couldn't cry because I knew it would make Mom sadder, and although she was strong during the day, I could hear her sobbing in bed at night. In her sleep she would call out my father's name, "Ray, Ray, Rayyyyyy."

I missed our house almost as much as I missed my father.

He was so much a part of it. He was so much a part of my whole world.

Many years later when I was in my thirties, I was driving down 38th Street in my old maroon Plymouth, Mother bouncing along by my side in the passenger seat. Street lights punched holes in the darkness. The sound of crickets floated over the traffic and through our open car windows. Suddenly, Mom turned to me and said, "I never asked you how you felt about moving after Dad died. I've wondered sometimes how that was for you, leaving the house you grew up in."

This was what had been missing for me: that someone wanted to know how I felt, and that how I felt mattered. Even though the question came twenty years after we moved, it was food that fed my hunger to be heard. Real food. Oatmeal, not Twinkies. I began to tell Mom how I did feel then, and how much I appreciated her asking, especially how much I appreciated her asking. But I got too close to raw emotion. She looked ahead at the street, the night, the cars. "I wonder what they're doing over there on Pleasant Avenue. They've been working on that street all summer," she mused.

It was brief, but one moment like that, one authentic

moment makes you realize that what your soul hungers for is real. You know then that you can tell when you get what you need, like a flower knows water. That one tiny moment is life dancing with you, and the music is fine. Being able to speak what is in your heart is the heart of being alive.

A few days after the sweat, I took a road trip to Taos, New Mexico. As I sped down Colorado State 285 through the San Luis Valley, with sagebrush as far as the eye could see on the right and the Sangre de Cristo mountains on the left, I thought about the Native American giveaway ceremony. The giveaway (*Otirhan* in Lakota) means that you are always willing to give away what you own. It keeps you from making things too significant. Giving things away allows you to live in freedom. You don't hang on to things.

Waiting for chances to speak and be heard, I saw that I had been hanging on to my words. I didn't want to be ignored or laughed at, so I became guarded. I disappeared inside myself. I'd speak and then forget what I had said, as if the words were leaves blown away on the wind.

What if I could find my voice only by giving the words away? What if the stories that eluded me must be given to others who will try them on and maybe wear them, maybe cast them off?

As the highway passed beneath me, I thought about how, in the sweat lodge, in the dark, all voices became one voice, like strands in a web. Each voice spoke her truth, yet there was a part of each woman's words that fit each one of us. I began to hear in the voices the voice of life, the sacredness of all experience. What if mine is just a voice? Not *my* voice, but *a* voice, weaving a part of a much greater whole? What if I gave that part away?

I thought about the things we had spoken of—birth, children, passion, loss, our bodies. We spoke of being women. Some of us spoke of loving men, some of being abused by men. We spoke of the earth and how the earth is deeply feminine, a fertile, breathing body that ebbs and flows with the cycles of the seasons. We saw that abusing the earth and abusing women are intricately connected, and that for both women and men to recover the sacred feminine is to heal ourselves and the planet.

We hadn't yet spoken about age. During the last round of the sweat, I asked, "Please assist my mother on her journey into spirit with your love, and pray that the time she has left here on earth be full and joyful." "Yes," the women murmured, "Yes" like a swelling wave. "We are with her. We send her our love." My mother in the lodge completed the circle. All the elders were present, my mother the representative.

As night fell, I thought about the visions I had received in the moist blackness of the lodge. That the sweat would take me deep into the stories that speak my life filled me with awe. But it was the next step for a now grown child, who often felt like a little seedling pushing its thin green shoot through hard ground, reaching, reaching with my poems and stories for sunlight and water. Then whomp, the crushing foot of silence or criticism. No fruit. No flower. I had sunk roots for a long, long time, tapping the stories I thought no one wanted to hear.

Being in Colorado in the spring gave me distance. So have the years since the days of my silence. I have more compassion now. I see that not being able to express her love and her concern cost my mother a great deal. I see that she loved, nevertheless, as fully and fiercely as she knew how. I have faced the seventh direction, the center, and opened my heart.

Shortly after I returned to my home in Minneapolis, Mom started talking about things she had never talked about before. "Are you happy?" she asked on the way back from a Mother's Day gathering at my sister's house. All that day her thoughts had been disjointed. Now they were clear, her manner urgent. "I want you to know that you were the most special. You came so late in my life." A little later that evening at my house, she said, "You were always different from the others. Deep." She used words I had never heard her use before. "I didn't always connect the circle," she said, "so I didn't understand your poems and your stories. But they were beautiful. I am proud of you."

Still later that night when I took her home, she would not go into her apartment, but ran through the halls of her building knocking on doors shouting, "Call the police. Call the police." I called 911 for an ambulance. "I haven't lived here in years," she informed the ambulance driver, "and my daughter is trying to hurt me." After several hours in the emergency room, she was released to a small nursing home, but we knew then that she had Alzheimer's disease and she would continue to decline.

I have met my voice in the voices of the women in the lodge. I have reclaimed my stories by opening my heart and being willing to give the stories away. I know my truth and I speak my truth. I speak for the women and the men, the elders and the children. I speak for the earth and all her creatures. I speak from the wisdom of the dark, moist places. I give voice to what it is to be human, to be woman, to love, to feel.

I am Lynn, daughter of Dorothy, granddaughter of Emma and Louise, mother of Louise and Shannon, grandmother of Jackae and Charmaine.

ALL MY RELATIONS.

I Speak from the Wisdom of the Dark, Moist Places

Finding Your Stories

1. List five things you haven't done because you are afraid.

2. List five things you were afraid to do, but you did them anyway.

3. What are the advantages of stopping when you are afraid? The disadvantages?

4. What are the advantages and disadvantages of moving forward through your fear?

5. When do you feel most connected with all that exists? Most disconnected?

6. Tell a story about one of your parents.

7. Tell a story about stepping into another culture.

8. Tell a story about stepping into another world.

9. Tell about an animal that you feel drawn to. Trust that
   there is a reason you chose this animal. Tell about it with
   imagination and relish.

II
Trusting Your Stories

rusting your stories means trusting your life. Once you muster the courage, the sense of humor, or simply the awareness it takes to awaken a life story—and tell it from your unique point of view—it will reflect back to you more than you saw when you first brought it to light. Like finding a stone on the beach, something about a particular story catches your eye. As you wet it, dry it, polish it, and pay attention to it, the story reveals its facets. "Oh," you marvel. "Oh! I didn't realize its true beauty."

Trust the creative process

Trusting the natural creative process is key to trusting your stories. You don't always know where a story is going to lead. So just letting it rip, stumbling through it, getting something down, is one way to trust. Don't even think about editing yet. Start letting your raw material surface in whatever form it takes. This valuable raw material runs right to the mother lode.

When you first begin to connect with your stories, you might get the feeling that they are in short supply, that the story you are working with is the last one that will ever come to you. This happened to me when I was writing "Reunion at Creation Lake" on page 107. The words and images, it seemed, were delivered to me personally by my own private muse; they flowed effortlessly onto the page. It was a miracle I feared would never happen again. I mumbled about this to a professor I had at the time who wisely responded, "You are arrogant to think that what comes to you is your doing. You must open yourself up and trust. You are but the vehicle." I have never forgotten those words.

The creative process begins by being willing to begin, by opening yourself, and by being willing to not know how it will turn out.

You can build trust in your creative process by playing

with the perspectives from which you tell a story. When you first find a story, you tell it the way it comes out. At this stage, you have probably not named it, but you have a point of view or perspective that influences the course of the story.

To broaden and deepen your story, name the perspective from which you are telling, then tell it again from a completely different perspective. In doing this, you will find that your stories aren't that rare and delicate. You will realize they will not slip from your grasp. Instead, you will see that they are resilient. They are malleable. They are like fresh sourdough bread; many good loaves will rise from the same starter.

An easy way to play with perspective is to use a tool I call the Story Wheel. Here is what it looks like:

To explain how this actually works, look at "The Dog Leash and Divine Order" on page 181. As it stands, I tell the story from a Spiritual perspective. What if I told it from a Friends perspective? Maybe I would emphasize my disappointment in never seeing Katherine again. If I told it from a Community perspective, I might talk more about the Essenes of old and how we make communities in the modern world—or don't. If I were to tell this same story from a Health perspective, I might emphasize Katherine's work as a midwife or the health benefits of not stressing over a stuck dog leash. You can see the possibilities.

The beauty of playing with perspective is twofold. One is that it allows you to relax in the knowledge that your story has an essential strength that lends itself to the loving hand of creation. The other is that looking at a story from different angles, one at a time, reveals underlying themes that provide choices or embellishments you wouldn't have access to otherwise.

Trust the voice that tells your stories

Some of you are natural storytellers whose authentic voices speak from your true center. Others have to practice, like I do, not filtering your experience through the eyes or opinions of others. Storytelling helps us listen to and trust the clarity and rightness of our own voices.

I began writing this section on trusting your voice while enjoying a cappuccino at a coffeehouse near my home. I spread my notes over the little metal table, trying to tune the other patrons out as I fretted over what to say about voice and how to say it. The topic, though dear to my heart, felt abstractly uninteresting. I wrote and sipped. I ate a chocolate mint cookie. I got very serious and wordy trying to explain how to trust your voice. In the midst of it all, I overheard my neighbor Rachel having a spirited conversation with her five-year-old daughter, Mara, who was eating a sprinkle dough-nut at the table behind me.

"I can sing better than Judy Garland because I'm not dead," declared Mara. The quirky freshness of her observation penetrated my lofty thoughts. I laughed. I paused. Mara's words made me realize that although I can hardly carry a tune in a bucket, I, too, can sing better than Judy Garland because I'm not dead either. Mara's unfiltered wisdom tapped into something universal in me: gratitude for life, a reminder to laugh—and a new way to look at my singing voice. Just as I was scratching away at my notebook, not trusting the flow or my voice one bit, Mara gave me this story to illustrate what it is to trust your voice.

Listen to people who have not yet learned to distrust their voices. Most of them will be very young. You will learn a lot. Trust the river of *your* voice. Do not edit for a while. To do so is to place your attention where it doesn't belong if you are to grow in trust.

Trust the evolutionary process

Once you have played with the Story Wheel and you have chosen a perspective from which to tell your story, trust the evolutionary process that follows. A story might go through many incarnations. It might come alive, then go dormant for a while as you lose interest in it. Or it grows slowly, like the good old oak that guards your house. Or once in a while, a story might spring forth whole and alive in the first telling. All you do after that is take care of it like a bright-eyed newborn.

If you are telling your story to an audience, when you look out and connect with the people before you, you will see their emotion and feel their responses. In trusting the evolutionary process, you dance, so to speak, with your story, adding or changing elements as you respond to the energy of your audience. You begin to trust that you will honor the essence of the story while molding it a little differently each time you tell it. You begin to trust your ability to be present in the moment—to yourself, to your story, and to your listeners.

As you will see from the stories that follow, trust is a recurring theme for me. On the one hand, I implicitly trust the abundance of life and the process of finding stories. On the other hand, I get amnesia often enough to have to learn the lessons of trust many times over.

Reunion at Creation Lake

A metaphorical story about trusting your voice

They had just had a falling-out, and Witchbaby had to drive all the way to Creation Lake with Exactomama. Exactomama sulked, having read just a few days earlier entries from a journal that Witchbaby kept hidden behind her bed so no one would find it. Exactomama called Witchbaby a traitor, not family, someone who knows nothing about love. "You can't write what you feel, Witchbaby. Words written are forever, and if you forget you slashed me to bits on your private pages, I copied the words on a napkin so their edges will stay sharp."

Witchbaby drove in silence, gripping the wheel, swallowing her words until they arrived at the lake. She knew Noright Sorrysister would be coming to the reunion, and Noright would say the apology prayer.

Exactomama stiffly opened the car door and stepped onto the manicured lawn of the cozy resort. Sisters flew from cabin doors to greet their mama and their youngest sister.

"It's been so long!"

"We don't get together nearly often enough!"

"When is the last time we talked? I mean really talked?"

"Mama, are you all right?"

"I'm fine," Exactomama replied tersely. She believed that terseness and strength were the same thing. She never burdened anyone with her troubles, preferring the nobler suffering of silence.

Noright Sorrysister knew Exactomama was mad; she always knew those things. "Did you go and write something Mama didn't like again?" she asked Witchbaby. "Mama taught you to keep your mouth shut, didn't she? And she taught you well, I might add. The good Lord should have given you the sense to hold your tongue. Hiding what you feel isn't good enough. Don't say it—on paper or anywhere else."

"But it was my journal, Noright. I have a right to speak in my own journal. It's Mama who has no right . . . "

"Don't you say one more word about Mama after all she's done for you, Witchbaby," scolded Noright. "I'm going to find Exactomama right this minute and set things right. See to it that you don't embarrass us this weekend with any comments about life as you know it. All I want is for this reunion to go smoothly. Grow up, kid, and face reality."

Noright spent the afternoon making up litanies. Exactomama sat on a lawn chair facing the lake, growing fat on sorry crumbs. The afternoon air smelled of offerings.

Witchbaby brushed flies off the screen door of one of the cabins, opened the door a crack, and slid into a musty kitchen before the flies could get in. Ladytidy Apronsister was on her hands and knees spreading waxen words on the well-worn floor with a cloth.

"Any beer?" Witchbaby called.

"In the fridge," Ladytidy mumbled. "Help yourself. And bring some out to the others. I won't be out until I get this place cleaned up. God, what a mess."

"But Ladytidy, you're on vacation. Come out and build castlepoems with me. Just like when we were little. We'll take turns being queen. The waves will make our music. The trees will dance to our words. Don't be like that, Ladytidy. Please."

"Witchbaby," sniffed Ladytidy, "won't you ever grow up and face reality? Things need to be done. After everything is done, everything needs to be redone. That is quite enough to keep anyone busy, I should think, and there are very satisfying rewards for busyness."

Witchbaby took a long drink from her bottle of beer. The bubbles burst in her mouth like Ladytidy's words, stinging. It was too hot to argue.

Out on the back lawn sat Whisper Silencesister, all alone eating cookies. From a very young age, Whisper had swallowed everything. She swallowed sounds, stories; sometimes she swallowed whole days and nights and even streets and cities. Witchbaby believed that, now, a whole universe lay unborn in Whisper's belly. She watched her most loved sister from a distance and felt sad as her sister's belly grew larger and larger. Whisper's time had come long ago, but she still sat alone under a tree releasing one word per month from alternate ovaries.

Witchbaby crossed the lawn and sat down quietly next to Whisper. The sisters embraced, one swallowing her sobs, her tears, the other roaring like a great tornado, her tears filling Creation Lake so full that Exactomama had to move her chair back from the rising water. "I will deliver you, sister. I will deliver you!" Witchbaby cried.

Whisper's throat began to contract. The words that lay in her belly had given form to what was essential in her, twisting and bonding like helixes. "Push, sister, push. Everything is all right. I am here. I am here with you," coaxed Witchbaby.

Whisper's mouth began to dilate. "Yes. You've known it all the time, Whisper. Yes." And with a scream as haunting as the cry of a thousand loons, Whisper gave birth to the moon and the stars.

Ladytidy wrung her hands moaning, "Babies make such messes."

Noright crowed, "You'll pay for this." And to Mama she spat, "Whisper should have had an abortion."

Exactomama grunted, "Illegitimate."

For the rest of the weekend, everyone but Witchbaby and Whisper acted like nothing had happened. After the picnic on Sunday afternoon, the two sisters said their good-byes to the family, and slipped away to spend a few enchanting hours together. As the sun set over Creation Lake,

Witchbaby and Whisper promised each other they would keep in touch. Really.

Reunion at Creation Lake

Finding Your Stories

1. Sit still and turn your attention inward by taking several deep breaths. See if you can identify three to five different parts of yourself that you don't normally consider separate and distinct from the essence of your being. Maybe there is an aggressive part of you that wants it all; a timid part that hides in the shadows; a perfectionist that wants to set the standards. Names these characters, including your essence, and make up a story about them.

2. Remember when you were a child and played with dolls, toy soldiers, action figures, or model horses? Go to a store that sells little plastic figures—dinosaurs, cowboys, robots, etc.—and pick out several pieces. Play with them and see what story emerges. Make props like a mountain, a forest, a bridge, a body of water to add to the fun.

3. Do the previous exercise with one or two other people.

The Package that Came for Shirley

S hirley used to live downstairs in the duplex where I still live upstairs. We shared this home on Pillsbury Avenue for ten years, good friends and sisters under the skin. In 1990, when Shirley decided it was time to buy a larger house that would accommodate her growing brood of grandchildren, I bought her half of the duplex, redid the hardwood floors and installed my beauty salon in what used to be her living room.

Shirley had been gone a year, but she still came back for

haircuts and perms. One August, the day before she had a hair appointment, a small cardboard box addressed to Shirley Joy Shaw arrived in the mail. It had no return address, but was carefully taped, typed, and stamped. I guessed it was some kind of advertising gimmick and almost threw it away as I did her other junk mail. "Those lists never die," I muttered to myself, but decided that since she would be there the next day, I ought to save it.

Shirley called having a perm "getting my natural curl back." This took time. After the rods were in and saturated with solution, I brought out the box. "This came for you yesterday," I said handing it to her. "Looks like that tree seedling promotion that my beauty supply company did a while ago. Need a boxed baby pine for your yard?"

We were both curious. "No return address. That's strange," said Shirley as she turned the box over and over, looking for a clue to its origin. I gave her an old scissors so she could cut the tape. Inside were layers of tissue paper carefully folded around something she had to dig to get to. We knew it wasn't a pine seedling, but there was no letter or anything else to indicate who it was from or why it had been sent. When she came to the inner layer, she could feel a small, hard object inside. She slid it out of the last piece of tissue.

"Lynn, this is the ring I lost when I lived in Paris in 1969." She held it up, a small gold band set with diamonds and rubies. "It belonged to my grandmother. One day it just disappeared. It was a keepsake that meant the world to me. I looked all over for it." We each sucked in our breath, letting this register. "You mean twenty-some years ago you lost this ring in Paris," I said, "and here it is, sent to an address you no longer live at, but the day before you come over here the ring arrives and there you are?" We examined the box again for some sign of where it had from; we unfolded the tissue paper piece by piece in hope of finding a name or a note. A St. Paul postmark was the only hint, and that led us nowhere.

We had both heard of stories about spoons floating through walls and other mysterious manifestations. We had read about strange things happening to other people, but this was too close to home. Shirley had expected to go home with curl in her hair, not her grandmother's ring on her finger.

When Shirley's Grandma was alive, she lived on Birch Lake near Ely, Minnesota, on land bought with money she made selling corsets door to door. I have been to that land with Shirley. I have come home replenished.

Many days the west wind washes the shore of that land

with low lapping waves until early evening—then stillness. No sound but the birches picking up the breath of a breeze like gossips swearing not to tell, and one loon cries from the other side of Grandma's island, just the distance of a good swim from the shore in front of the cabin. Many days the wind howls and the trees bend, the waves whip against the dock and the silence is broken by the voice of the wilderness dancing to the drumming of the thunder gods. No day is alike, yet there is a continuity that a sense of place gives you over time. Grandma got to know that place and love it. So did Shirley.

The land had an old trappers cabin on it where Grandma stayed during the summer. Eventually, she built a new cabin, a house really, starting with the kitchen and adding each room separately, year by year, until she declared it finished. An entryway full of fishing gear and enamel basins leads into the kitchen where Grandma's formidable white enamel woodstove still demands homage for the hot doughnuts it once fried in deep iron pans. There are two side rooms in a lean-to off the kitchen, with ceilings so low you must duck your head. Today the rooms store air mattresses and bright orange life jackets, but once, the smallest of the two rooms, barely five feet by ten feet, held a cot for Shirley's grandpa.

Shirley says he planted flowers around the house every summer until it became too painful for him to stay. But he had his whiskey and a house in nearby Virginia, Minnesota. When Grandma married the land, she never really left Grandpa. She just let him go.

Grandma was a touchstone in Shirley's life, giving her a reverence for nature and a sense of adventure. Grandma fed Shirley the kind of love her mother couldn't give. It wasn't only the hot, homemade doughnuts. It was, despite Grandma's Scandinavian reserve, her heart that held the little girl firmly. And it was the lake outside the door and the wide Birch River that flows into the lake at the rocky split down the path, and it was the impenetrable woods that border Superior National Forest, along with the singing, impulsive wind, that carried Shirley home to Grandma's every summer.

When Shirley's grandma died, she left a legacy of love that lives on in a grown woman's remarkable work with elderly people. Shirley's grandma was the inspiration for Rakhma Homes, small shared homes "with a heart" that house and care for frail elderly people with the dignity and love that Grandma lived. Home is what Grandma gave Shirley. Home is what Shirley gives others.

Strange as it was to find that package in the mail, it seemed natural and right that Grandma's ring came home, too.

The Package that Came for Shirley

Finding Your Stories

1. When you tell about something, you relate details like a report. When you tell stories, you raise questions that engage the listener. (Most likely, the questions engage you, too, for no matter how good a story is in and of itself, you must be passionate about it; you must be involved with it somehow to make it come alive.) It is very interactive, even though the listener may not respond verbally. A story raises questions right toward the beginning. "What is in the package?" is the big question in this story. "Why did it come now?" is another one. "Where did it come from?" is another. Look at one or two stories that you like and see what questions they raise. Are the questions answered by the end of the story?

2. What are the questions of your life, your themes, your obsessions? Write them down. These are the bigger questions that will

help you select your stories, or shape them to reflect your themes. For instance, if one of your themes is loss, you might tell a story about standing on the shore watching a ship sail toward the horizon and disappear into the mist, never to be seen again. If one of your themes is return, you may tell a similar story, only the ship reappears on a new horizon, a small dot taking shape as it sails toward those waiting on another shore.

3. Tell about a mystery that was never solved.

4. Where is home for you? Is it a place? A feeling? Certain people? Tell a story about returning home, or about something that returned home.

The Candy Jar Diet

E very day after school, Maggie Holman and I made hot
fudge sauce from her mother's recipe to drizzle gener-
ously over vanilla ice cream that lay waiting in the back
of her mother's freezer. We had to cook the sauce just right so
that when the hot fudge hit the cold scoops it would harden
and almost crack. We chewed the buttery strands as the ice
cream slipped down our throats, and we always had more.
Then we would go upstairs to Maggie's room, turn sideways
in the full-length mirror, and bemoan how fat we were.

Like many women, I became ensnared in the thinner-is-
better trap early in high school. For me it was my stomach.

It wasn't flat. Never mind that I was 5'9" and skinny. I had a round stomach; I was fat. Worrying about being too fat turned into an obsession that ran my life until I discovered the "candy jar diet" many years later.

I ate grapefruits and eggs. I ate 600 calories a day. I sneaked food in private when no one was looking. Sometimes I ate whole bags of Oreo cookies. I abhorred myself for doing that. I fasted. I rode my bicycle three times around Lake Harriet to make up for the extra bowl of oatmeal I ate for breakfast. I took karate lessons and worked out five times a week. I walked. I ran.

I woke up in the morning thinking about what to have for breakfast, lunch, and dinner, always running a calorie tab from the day before. I did prophylactic eating, making sure that if a meal was going to be late, I could eat something to prevent future hunger. I talked constantly about dieting with my friends, most of whom shared my love of food and fear of fat. "I'll just have a salad," I would announce breezily at the restaurant, "with a little French on the side." Then I'd go home and privately inhale a bag of chocolate chips.

In 1976 I read *Fat Is a Feminist Issue* by Susie Orbach. That year, as part of a university course I was taking, I did a project requiring oral and written presentation of any topic

I chose. Being completely stuck on the diet-binge-diet merry-go-round, I chose to research compulsive eating. I used my life experience as a point of reference and *Fat Is a Feminist Issue* as a point of departure.

Orbach's main premise is that diets don't work because they deprive. They say to women, You are not good enough, pretty enough, feminine enough the way you are. You must deprive yourself of food/nurturing/pleasure/self-definition to be worthy of a mate/nice clothes/being taken seriously/a fulfilling life. When we are deprived, we crave what we cannot have.

That didn't make sense to me until I did this little exercise: Try not to think of chocolate chip cookies, Lynn. You may not have them anymore. Try really hard not to think of chocolate chip cookies. Don't think of lemon meringue pie, either. For that matter, just quit thinking of anything that contains sugar . . . What did "don't think of" conjure up? The exact cookie I instructed myself to ignore, fresh from the oven with the chocolate, gooey inside. Mile-high meringue with tart lemon filling that makes each bite a delight to the tongue. You get the picture.

So what else is there besides The Diet? Orbach talked about giving ourselves permission to have our hungers. To let ourselves know what we are hungry for and how much.

To eat when we are hungry and stop when we are full. To start listening to ourselves, not to some external definition of ourselves. How can we know what we are hungry for if we don't trust our own bodies as they are? How can we know what our bodies want if we listen only to the "food experts"? How can we know how much is enough if we rely on pre-scribed portions from the diet of the month rather than on listening to our own miraculous body wisdom?

For a few months prior to doing my project, I had been meeting with an entity named Evangeline. She was a spirit who spoke through my friend Michael Macmacha and had been his grandmother in her last lifetime. I had sessions with Michael regularly in which he went into an altered state so that Evangeline could come through. Evangeline described her work as that of midwife. The first time I spoke to her she said, "I'm usually not lethal." I asked, "What do you mean usually?" She replied, "I only kill the false self."

She told me that in whatever dimension we live, we have our work. There are beings like herself on the other side who work in the realm of consciousness. Their job is to open channels of awareness to those of us on the physical plane.

Many work behind the scenes, never making direct physical contact with human beings, and there are some like Evangeline who bridge the worlds by speaking through people living among us.

Evangeline's mission was to midwife the true self. She was a gentle, loving guide who allowed me to start wherever I was and go from there. When I started seeing her, I was mostly thinking about food and disliking my body. At one session, I told her I was planning a solo winter stay at a friend's cabin the next weekend. She said, "Be sure you bring doughnuts." I said, "I had planned on fasting the whole time." She said, "Bring doughnuts and other things you like." I squirmed in my chair, afraid to be with myself and a bag of doughnuts and other things I liked for a whole weekend. She knew that but thought it would be a good idea anyway.

It was hard but I took the goodies. That was the beginning of a new awakening to what it's like to have permission to eat. I was no longer just thinking about it like a good idea from a book. I was actually being encouraged to do the thing I knew would send me over the edge and spin me out of control forever. In deprivation you are a prisoner with no freedom to choose. You must be constantly vigilant. One slip and you're done.

Evangeline taught me about awareness and permission. That weekend at the cabin was the beginning of a long birthing process. It was the first contraction. I just noticed myself in my own company with food in the house and no one around to cook it for or to look over my shoulder as I ate. I had all I could do to be with myself, looking over my own shoulder the whole weekend.

Though there was a lot more to learn, I began to realize that awareness was key. Orbach talked about charting feelings while eating, times of day, looking at whether the eating occurred in response to hunger or something else. Did we stop to find out the exact thing we were hungry for? What did we say to ourselves when we ate? What did we think about food? How had we made it sacred or mysterious? Could we throw it away or push it around with our noses? Why not?

As the class progressed and the project came together, I decided that this material had the potential for such healing that I needed to create a food and body image group for women. With guidance from the book and an extensive background in group dynamics, I ran a prototype group that proved to be extraordinary. After that first series, a psychotherapist named Liz Aronica joined me, and we collaborated for the next eight years presenting seminars, work-shops, and groups on food and body image called "Feeding the Woman in Ourselves." We addressed the spiritual starvation women often feel, the emptiness that cannot be filled with food. As we drew distinctions about our hungers, spiritual and physical, we gained a great deal of freedom.

It just so happened that Liz knew Evangeline, too, and had been seeing her occasionally herself. I told Liz about the work I had been doing with Evangeline on my own compulsive eating. By this time Evangeline had gone a lot further with me. Picking up on the themes of awareness and permission, Evangeline suggested I get a gallon glass jar like those found at food co-ops, one with a screw-on lid. I was to fill this jar with candy and keep it filled. I could eat as much candy as I wanted with one stipulation: Every time I had a piece, I had to unscrew the lid, reach in, take the candy, and screw the lid back on. Before the jar got even a little empty, I was to go down to the store, get more candy, and fill it to the brim.

This was too much to contemplate. How could I do that? I would become a distended blimp, filling first my kitchen, then the living room, then my whole house. I would never be able to stop. Never. This was the most ridiculous thing I had ever heard. Evangeline said it would make me aware.

I didn't see how, but I trusted Evangeline, so one day I went down to the co-op and bought a gallon glass jar. On the way home I stopped at the SuperValu and stocked up on jelly beans and peppermints and red licorice and M&M Peanuts and SweetTarts and Bit-O-Honeys and malted milk balls. When I got home, I tore open the bags and dumped all the candy into the jar. It was so pretty. I was so scared.

For an entire month I was in the jar all the time. Unscrew lid. Take piece of candy. Screw lid back on. Unscrew lid. Take piece of candy. Screw lid back on. I'd be down at the store almost every day buying another bag of orange marshmallow peanuts or Hershey Kisses or M&M Peanuts. Liz knew about the candy jar. I had her full support. Otherwise I would have panicked the first week, thrown it all in the garbage and started a diet—no, a fast. But this was no quick fix. It would take as long as it would take. My job was to just notice my hand unscrewing the lid, reaching in the jar, putting the candy in my mouth, screwing the lid back on the jar.

I began to notice something else. I was still eating a lot of candy, but about the only thing I went for after a while were the M&M Peanuts. I bought bags of them at the grocery store. Even though there was other candy in the jar, if I was out of the M&M Peanuts, I didn't want the other stuff. That was a big change. I never used to care. I just ate candy. I ruminated for a few days about this. Then it hit me. "It must be the nuts my body wants! Why else would I be leaving the rest?" So I went down to the co-op, bought a few more jars with lids that screwed on and off and filled them up with different kinds of nuts. I let myself eat nuts any time I wanted. Eventually I got tired of nuts. I began to crave ice cream.

I went down to the SuperValu and bought enough ice cream to fill my freezer. I found a few vanilla fudge crumb bars too. I questioned my sanity often, but I had begun to see the possibilities of giving myself permission to eat with awareness. Now, when I ate the ice cream, which I did anytime I wanted, I would walk around the house saying things like, "I can have all the ice cream I want. I can have all the love I want. I can have all the sex I want. I can have all the pleasure I want. I can have all the ice cream I want." I loved the vanilla fudge crumb bars so much that I'd buy five or six at a time. A few days later, I'd go get more. When my craving for those subsided, I hardly bought any more, and the store quit carrying them. I must have been a market unto myself.

The outcome of all this is that I have freedom with food.

I am no longer obsessed by my cravings for food or my fear of it. I have found ways not only to nurture myself with food, but to attend to the big hunger, the spiritual hunger that couldn't be filled. I never thought I would be able to say that. I have learned that you can't say no freely, to food or anything else, unless you can say yes freely. Without the freedom to say yes, no is not a choice. It is an imposition that the true self will wrestle with in all kinds of wily ways, creating a vicious circle that strangles self-expression and authenticity, keeping us spiritually starved.

It has been more than twenty years since I had my candy jar. It was a metaphor for my life. I had been living as if there was only one piece of candy in the candy jar. Only one piece of love. Only one good job. Only one chance to be a good mom. My whole world had been one of self-deprivation. Even though there was abundance all around, I didn't allow myself.

I lived a rich and full life. But instead of savoring the sweetness, I held back. I always needed to justify my enjoyment. Oh, this trip is for work. Oh, a night at the theater—I'm working on a project at school and we have to go. Oh, a good man to love me? He has two kids. It would never work. In truth, I was afraid I would lay into the richness like a starving vulture going for blood. I would make a fool of myself. I would go out of control.

I saw, with the candy jar, that my body was trustworthy; she tells me what she wants, how much she wants, and when she is full. When my body knows she can have anything she wants, she self-regulates. The candy jar taught me to embrace all my appetites like I embraced my appetite for food. It taught me that I could trust my sexuality, my need for love, my need for rest and exercise, and my ability to say yes and no. The candy jar taught me that I could trust myself.

The funny thing about awareness is that you can't practice it "so that." You can't use it as another fix. "I'll become aware of what I eat so that I will lose weight." "I'll pay attention to how I speak so that people will listen." The paradox is that awareness brings freedom but not if used as a technique. It is simply a way of being that allows us to see things as they are. As we are willing to be present to things as they are, they can change, naturally.

The Candy Jar Diet

Finding Your Stories

1. Think of a person you don't like. How does she dress? What does her voice sound like? How does she behave? How do you listen to him? Can you trust him? Develop a story character you can't trust.

2. Trust your body. Trust your voice. This, we are told, is the ticket to self-knowledge and authentic self-expression. But is it possible to trust yourself if you don't like yourself? Many women learn early on not to like themselves very much. The messages that we are not enough and/or too much are both blatant and subtle. What are some of the messages you carry about being a woman? If you are a man, what are the messages you carry about women? About your own feminine side? Where do the messages come from?

3. Let's look again at strategy. "How-to" books are written by the millions. Articles in every magazine give us techniques for improving everything from our self-esteem to our sex lives. We still fall short. Strategy doesn't work because it is another fix. We can strategize our whole life—how to win, how to look better, how to lose weight, how to feel better, how to get our children to behave. But strategy is a thing to do. Without awareness, without just letting the condition be fully and completely as it is, doing something to change it isn't going to make much difference.

For most people, the automatic response to awareness about something is "I don't like it, I have to change it." What if you just noticed, period? And just noticed some more? And just noticed some more after that?

4. What situation have you strategized to change? What strategies have you used? What has been the result? Are you willing to just be with the situation, noticing exactly how it is and how it isn't? Then notice how you respond to it, what physical sensations you have, what feelings come up, etc.? Do this for a period of time—a week or a month. See how awareness makes room for life as it is. See how it embraces what is instead of resists it. See the difference between change and transformation. Tell a story about this.

A Mother Waiting to Happen:
An Awakening to Trust

After telling one of my clients that I had just declared the upcoming year my Year of Creativity, a time for me to come back to the creative person I once was, she brought me *The Artist's Way, A Spiritual Path to Higher Creativity,* by Julia Cameron. A gifted and generous writer, Cameron takes you on a twelve-week journey into your soul. She calls it creative recovery. I call it creative rediscovery.

I spent the summer immersed in that book, revisiting parts of my life I had left behind, forgotten, or had just become resigned about. I looked at what I thought being creative meant, whom I had given my power to, how I had dismissed myself as an artist. I had forgotten to play, to take risks, to speak up for my creative self. And I got to see just how much I had to be in charge of everything so I could arrange my life to create—someday.

God is mentioned often in Cameron's book. If you don't relate to the word *God,* she suggests "good orderly direction," or any number of other names you may have for your higher power. "The point," she says, "is not what you name it. . . . You are seeking to forge a creative alliance, artist-to-artist with the Great Creator. Accepting this concept can greatly expand your creative possibilities."

I had always been fascinated by spiritual practices, religious thought, cultural and historic concepts of god and goddess. I practice yoga and meditation. I have studied Native American traditions and have participated in sweat lodge ceremonies. I conduct women's rituals. I spend time in nature. I was surprised to find, though, what a hard time I had with the concept of a Creator who wants me to create.

The chapter on abundance just about did me in. I had

reasoned that I couldn't possibly have enough time, money, good ideas, publishers, or audiences unless I strategized, organized, prioritized, fantasized, and worked a night job. Even if I could make it work, my family would probably laugh, leave me, or both.

One of the sacred rituals of the *Artist's Way* is the daily writing of morning pages. They are not intended to be "good" writing, nor are they to be done only by those whose art is writing. Before you do anything else in the morning, you simply write three pages in which you air your thoughts and clear your mind. The chapter on abundance suggests writing about "the god you do believe in and the god you would like to believe in."

"I don't trust anybody, not even God. Particularly not God," I wrote one day in my morning pages. I was stunned at the black and white of it. I saw in that entry how I had been relying solely on my own limited beliefs about the source of abundance, so I thought I had to work everything out myself before I could risk writing my first book. I felt alone and pretty cynical. I put my journal down and let my mind wander.

I remembered how my daughter Louise and I had spent practically her whole lifetime of twenty-four years at odds with each other. It was hard to reach her, to let her know how terribly much I loved her. She was angry that her father left when she was a baby. She was angry that her sister got so much of my attention. She was angry I didn't understand her better. She was angry we didn't have much money. She was angry I talked too much about things she would rather have left unsaid. She was angry and the thing she needed most, my love, could not penetrate the anger. She was a prickly pear daring me to try again.

My mind wandered to my many heartsick journal entries of years past that recorded my longing to do right by Louise as she was growing up. I remembered my frustration when I came up with just the right gift or just the right thing to say, and it turned out to be wrong. I remembered my many attempts at loving her in ways she could feel my love, and I remembered giving up trying anymore.

When Louise was twenty-three, she came back from a three-day seminar she had taken. She had softened. Her face was open again, almost like when she was a child playing on the swing set in the backyard. She spoke to me, not at me, and when I spoke to her, she listened.

Shortly after that, Louise was accepted into an exchange program at Akita University in Japan. She called to see if she could stay at my house the night before she was to leave, and if I would drive her to the airport the next day. It wasn't a demand as in the past. It was a simple, open question. It was easy for me to say, "Of course." I was thrilled.

I made up her bed with crisp, clean sheets. I fluffed her pillows. In the morning, I prepared pancakes for breakfast. We told jokes while we ate. We loaded her suitcases into the car and headed for the airport where we waited together for another hour before she boarded the 747. We were able to be together with such ease. Sitting in the airport McDonald's, Louise blurted out, "Mom, you're being such a good mom!"

There was a moment of silence while I let this sink in. I had always wanted her to feel my love. Now, with new openness, she felt the presence of a good mom. It was so easy for me to provide for her in that openness. I had been a mother waiting to happen. I had always been there.

"Louise, thanks for letting me be a mom to you," I replied. "I've had such a good time helping you get ready for Japan."

Could it be, I thought, that I had been interpreting God's steadfast presence as aloof and uncaring, just as Louise had interpreted mine for so many years? Had I been so blind that I could only see God from my limited perspective, a perspective that didn't allow God much scope? I was saying by my actions and my attitude, "God, you're not doing it right." "God, I know how this should go." "God, you're not really there for me and I can tell you all the reasons why I think that." "God, with so many other people to look after, how could you have time for me?"

Could it be that all along God had been waiting for me like I had been waiting for Louise? If all she had to do to experience my love was to let me be a mom, maybe all I had to do to experience God's abundance was to let God be God.

Wow, those morning pages are powerful!

My teeny-tiny way of being with the gracious abundance of The Great Creator had been vaporized. It was like suddenly having a picture window after looking through a keyhole, and, what's more, the window flew wide open.

Thanks to my daughter's willingness that day to receive her mother's abiding love, I now know that God has always been present and full of love for me, whether I noticed it or not. As I experience God as a reliable Source that is beyond my understanding, I can listen to my deepest heart and act with the confidence that, if I listen, I will be shown the way. It's hard to say just how this happened, but money is no longer a concern for me. I trust that what I need will be there as I do my right work in the world. I trust that people who do belong with me will be there and that I can let them come and go with love. I trust that there is enough time to do the things that call to me, and that my creative rhythms, though they may not be nine to five, are true for me.

A Mother Waiting to Happen

Finding Your Stories

1. There is a Zen saying, "Don't push the river," but how often we try! It's practically un-American to *allow* life to unfold, much less trust that it will unfold beautifully. Maybe that's because we really don't observe life, or the river, for that matter. We have our own ideas of how a person or situation should be, then we scramble to make our lives fit our ideas.

   Let's use the river as a metaphor for your life in this exercise. Think about rivers for a moment. You could talk about rivers, their properties and characteristics. You could remember rivers you've seen in the past. You could visualize rivers you've read about and would like to see. Go even deeper:

   - This week, find a river or a creek and sit by it. Go every day if you can. Just watch it and listen to it. See where it takes you. Surrender to it as it is.
   - Write about what you learned.

- Tell a story about what happened, or about something that flowed from your time by the river.

2. Tell a story about a time when you trusted someone or something.

3. Tell a story about not trusting.

Going Where I've Never Been: More About Trust

W hen I first discovered the book, *The Artist's Way*, by Julia Cameron, and before I began using it to teach my own classes on creativity, I met informally with a group of women who were blocked creatives. One summer day we gathered on my patio. I showed everybody the drum I was making and lamented that I wanted to paint designs on its taut white skins. But I couldn't because I was sure I would ruin them. After all, I am a writer, not an artist.

A painter whose work impressed me was in the group.

"Jan," I ventured, "would you help me design the artwork for my drum?"

"Sure," she said. "Go down to Art Materials and get a watercolor sketch book. While you're there, pick out a tin of watercolor pencils. Make marks in the sketchbook. Make designs. Make mistakes. Play."

My stomach knotted up. "Jan," I said, "you don't understand. I am not an artist. I will ruin the drum. You are an artist."

"No, Lynn, you don't understand," Jan shot back gently but firmly. "You are an artist. Go get your stuff."

Several days passed. I finally trudged down to the art store. I got the watercolor pencils and a large sketchbook. I brought them home. I was afraid to start. It felt kind of like singing in public—too messy, too loud.

But eventually I started, tentative at first. Make a mark. Oh, just like regular colored pencil. Dip it in water. Oh. It washes and blends. Add another color. Oh. Nuances and shades. I did that? More water softens, gives me subtle, translucent tones. Less water—vivid pulsating splashes.

One day I brought my sketchbook and pencils to Java Jack's, a neighborhood coffeehouse where I like to sit outside in the sun to write or read with a cup of cappuccino. I found a little table, spread out my things, and became oblivious to everything but the pencils, the page, and the paper cup of ice water for pencil dipping. I made squiggles. I made lines. The page turned into a supersonic eagle in blue-green flight, brown wings, and ether. When I did look up, I noticed a little sandy-haired girl standing a few feet away, staring at me with big brown eyes.

"Mommy, she is an artist," I heard her say, pointing at me.

"Shh," her mommy said. "Let her work."

I laughed inside. "Everybody knows I'm an artist except me," I thought. "I don't even know what I'm doing."

Before the little girl left, her mother came over and told me that someday her daughter wants to be an artist. Could I tell her where to get some pencils like mine for the little girl's birthday? I said, "Your daughter is an artist. Here's where you can get the pencils."

As I spent more time with my sketch pad, I began to use it for my writing too. Large, blank white pages. No lines. One day when I had taken a two-day retreat to a cabin in the northern Minnesota woods, I was writing about how hard it is to say no to certain people and situations. After writing a page or two, I noticed I was going down a verbal drainpipe.

I got frustrated with the words. I didn't want to talk about this anymore. I just wanted to understand it.

I picked up my watercolor pencils and began to paint what NO looks like instead. I was amazed. My hand knew what to do. Soon there was a large, open heart in the middle of a bright blue globe. Roots grew down from the center of the heart. Lush green branches with delicate pink blossoms sprouted from the top. On the left of the globe, outside of it, a dark brown barrier pulsated, curving with the curve of the globe. The right side had no barrier. When I was done, I saw that for me, a person who says yes automatically—to be nice—saying no would allow me to open my heart. I saw that I could not say yes freely if I could not say no freely. No does not wall me off but allows me to grow and flower, to sink roots deep into life. I saw that always being available kills me like a field that never lies fallow is killed. I was awed by the clarity of the image I had painted, and how the words came later to describe what it told me.

Much later that evening, I brought out my drum and a kit of acrylics I had borrowed from a friend in case I got brave. As dusk fell, I painted my drum. I was scared, but I knew it was time. The acrylic paints were much different from the watercolor pencils. Some of them were hard and dry. I couldn't use them. I had to create what I wanted with the colors that were still moist. I went ahead, blending the colors of this unfamiliar medium on a pallet of wax paper. Amazingly, I knew how to paint and blend with the acrylics, too.

When I was done with the original design, I stepped back and looked at it. Hmmm . . . there was still something missing. With a wide brush, I added a circle of gold, blending yellow and orange on the wax paper pallet, sweeping the brush boldly around the edge of the drum head. There. The circle of the sun, the open heart protected by freedom to say yes or no, surrounded by light, illumination, and strength.

For a long time before this, my creativity was about the only thing I had said no to, and it wasn't freely. I said no to being openly creative out of fear of exposing myself. "Who does she think she is?" I could imagine friends and family snickering to each other. For so long I had been saying, "Yes, I'll get through school. Yes, I'll be successful at a real job. Yes, I'll have coffee with you, even though I need this time to write. Yes, I'll read one more book, take one more workshop, then I'll be ready." I didn't want to say, "No, I'm not like you. No, I cannot go today, I have a date with myself. No, I need nothing more to get ready. I am ready."

Sometimes I want to retreat from claiming my artist self,

the writer, the painter, the singer, the dancer in me. But once committed, I find I cannot go back. I can only trust, as Jan did, that what I need will come, that the universe will support my courage to take action.

Sometimes I want to scream out, "This was a fluke!!! That drum I painted; it happens only once. It was dumb luck. That story I wrote that came through me like lightening. What if there are no more stories like that in me? What if what I create is very, very bad?"

But by the time I have a drum to paint or a story to tell, it's too late. It's out of my hands. I have said yes to something that calls to me from the essence of my being. I have said yes to myself. How it turns out is not up to me. I just keep going and surrender to the process as if it were a fascinating lover. "Yes, yes," I say with all my heart, and go where I've never been before.

Going Where I've Never Been

Finding Your Stories

1. List five things you would like to say no to but can't.

2. List five things you would like to say yes to but haven't because you are doing so many things you wish you could say no to.

3. Get a sketchbook and a set of watercolor pencils and play.

4. Use other methods of expression besides words.
   - Sing a feeling
   - Dance a situation in your life
   - Create an image from clay, stone, wood, or metal to explore a question you've been grappling with.

5. Tell a story about surrender.

Hole in the Day

There is a lake near Brainerd, Minnesota, named Hole in the Day. Ever since my family and I drove past Hole in the Day Lake while on vacation, I have been thinking about what a hole in the day would be like. I have since learned that native people called a solar eclipse a hole in the day. But for me, a hole in the day is an eclipse of linear time.

I f there were a hole in the day, I would see yellow daisies by the side of the road. I would stop. I would pick some daisies and wear one in my hair, even though it is short and curly and doesn't blow in the wind.

If there were a hole in the day, a visitor would come and sit at my kitchen table unannounced. The white curtains would wave their welcome in the warm breeze. We would tell stories and laugh and drink lemonade. She would go home a little later, but she would leave her laughter with me. The music of her voice would rock me to sleep that night.

If there were a hole in the day, I'd make love like no one has ever made love before. My lover would come to me. "Put your things down," he would say. I would think, "I can't stop now. I am busy." But, like a morning glory opening to the sun, I would open to my lover, and he would show me the hole in the day. It would be like a velvet dress, with the velvet on the inside. It would be like fresh red raspberries that you picked yourself, the juice staining your fingers and your lips. It would be the longest, sweetest jewel of time outside of time. From then on, we would know the entrance into the hole in the day. We would go there often, and when I was eighty, I would look back and say, "I was not so busy after all."

If there was a hole in the day, a breath would breathe me deep into the center of my heart. There I would take out paints I didn't know I knew how to use, and just start. I would write poems I didn't know how to rhyme. I would

dance dances that came to my feet not from the foxtrot classes I took in eighth grade, but from somewhere yet to be discovered in the hole in the day.

The hole in the day is time for the soul. It is seeing time,
trusting time. It can be a time of great energy or a time of deep
rest. It can reveal the hidden in the obvious. "Oh, I get it," you
marvel to yourself. "Love does make the world go round." You
are drifting off to sleep one night when this is made known to
you. You know in your bones that love is the source of every
atom's dervish dance. You feel how far-reaching this kind of
knowing is.

When you allow your own knowing, you enter the hole in
the day. You no longer need to know facts, although facts are
quite nice and serve their own purposes. That's knowing
things. Things you learn. You accumulate facts. You put
them together. This does not occur in the hole in the day.
The knowing of things occurs in the momentum of the
hours and the minutes, over time.

Knowing what you know comes from another place. You
drop down into the stillness of your soul. There is no arro-
gance to this kind of knowing. It is simply so. If your life
were a boat with a beautiful white sail, this knowing is the
wind that stirs you.

A hole in the day is at once mundane and mysterious. The daily becomes sacred, in the sense that you get the full, awesome view. Your daughter's face is so completely familiar that you think you know her inside and out. Yet one moment you look through the hole in the day and you see a young woman so vastly unknown to you that who she is takes your breath away. How you love her.

If I had a house on Hole in the Day Lake, the light would shine in prisms through my many windows. The tables and chairs would meet the light, like living things, and take on an inviting sheen and softness. The rugs would remind my feet of the earth, the hearth, my heart of truth. There would be a little sailboat that would take me back and forth between the hole in the day and the laundry list of things to accomplish, that list that continues to grow even as items get checked off one by one. The boat would land at my dock every time I forgot to take a moment in the middle of it all and be right here right now. I would hear a voice—so enchanting I would have to follow—calling me to sail quietly into the dancing light at the center of the hole in the day and come back to myself once again, refreshed.

Hole in the Day

Finding Your Stories

1. "The Hole in the Day" isn't really a story. It's a meandering. It doesn't really have a beginning, a middle, and an end. It doesn't have characters or a plot of any kind. But it's fun. And It's another way to exercise your story muscles. Ruminate about something that intrigues you. Let your imagination go. Use your senses, all of them, touch, sight, hearing, taste, smell. Where does it take you?

2. My friend Greg says that to create, one must spend a lot of time doing nothing. He says that time for the artist is rather like an egg: The down time is what cushions the fragile yolk; without it there is no chance for new life. When have you passed through the hole in the day? What was that time like? Where did you go? Who or what was there?

3. Another friend, Mary Kay, had cancer that went into remission for

some months. During that time, Mary Kay became very familiar with the hole in the day. She called it God time. Interview someone who can tell you about non-linear time.

Lilacs Don't Bloom
in October

I t was time for a change. The crabgrass was out of control in the front yard and juniper bushes were rootbound beneath the sunporch window. But I am not a gardener. I kept letting the yard go year after year, and contented myself with the fact that at least it was green. When my neighbor, Douglas, who is a landscape designer, suggested installing flowers and plants indigenous to the Midwest and impervious to the Minnesota seasons, I agreed.

Douglas and I pored through catalogs of wildflowers. We

looked at trees that would shade the east windows in the summer and allow in the winter sun. We thought of the birds that could feed all winter on highbush cranberries. We chose flowering plants with names like Silky Aster, Pussytoes, and Midland Shooting Star, whose purples, pinks, yellows, and whites would undulate in ever-changing rainbows of color spring through fall.

Although I had lived in this house on 38th and Pillsbury for seventeen years and have loved lilacs since the day I moved in, I never planted a bush because I didn't want to wait for two or three years for it to bloom. Finally, with Douglas's encouragement, I got my lilac bushes.

They were tiny little things that spring, about knee-high. Five of them snaked across the north side of the yard flanked by irrepressible yellow daisies that sprang up and spread like scarves over a table that first summer. I knew I would have to wait for the lilacs. But I could imagine their perfume. I could see the nuances of color, deep purple to white. Vases of lilacs would dance through my rooms for springs to come.

One blustery October day, Douglas came over to pinch and prune my hearty, but still embryonic, garden. I was making tortellini in the kitchen when he called to me to come outside.

"There's a lilac on your bush," he said. "Come see."

"Douglas," I said. "Come on. I walk by those bushes every day. There are no lilacs out there. Lilacs don't bloom in October."

"So come on out and look," he insisted. "There is a lilac on your bush."

I turned off the stove, poured the steaming water off the pasta, and set it in a bowl. I followed Douglas out the front door. He led me over to the second bush.

"See," he said, cupping a small flower gently in his hand. And I saw it there, right by the sidewalk I had scurried up and down several times that day—a delicate, pale, fragrant lilac.

Impossible, I thought, even in the face of seeing it and touching it. But it wasn't impossible. And in that moment I not only saw the lilac, but I saw that maybe there is a whole world of things I know so much about that I don't even see what's there.

What about my daughters? I think I know them so well. What in my knowing of them keeps me from seeing them? And Bill, my life partner, my husband, the best man in the world. Do I look at him every day as if today is the first day

I am meeting him? What would I ask him? How would I listen if I didn't already know him?

What else do I say is impossible without looking beyond what I already know? That business I've dreamed of starting? The play I've thought of writing? Taking time for a trip to Arizona when the desert is in bloom? Maybe if I look with my eyes and my heart in the moment instead of with my memories of what I know from the past, maybe what is possible will take my breath away, like that little October lilac.

I went back inside, not to the sinkfull of dirty dishes that I had left a few minutes before, but to the most beautiful, fragrant, red tomato sauce that had ever been poured over tortellini.

Lilacs Don't Bloom in October

Finding Your Stories

1. Is there anything you've been putting off year after year? What is it and why do you put it off? How would things be different if you took action on this? Make a phone call. Pick up a pen. Dig a hole. Have it happen. Tell it as a story. Create different endings.

2. On public radio one day there was a story about a woman who had had a long bout with amnesia. She had been away from home for some time when her family found her. She returned home without memory of the past, a newborn in the familiar body of wife and mother. Life was a clean slate, a panorama of wonder and delight. Since she did not remember concepts like "mother," she cavorted with her teenage daughter, tried on makeup and listened to records with her, and even helped her get into trouble. Her daughter was startled and delighted.

Since the woman did not remember the concept of "sex" or any of her past training about it, her husband found her childish enthusiasm unexpectedly wild and funny. But it challenged his way of relating to her and to his own sexuality, and he didn't quite know how to deal with his "new" and playful partner.

- What would happen if you "forgot" how to be with someone you have a predictable relationship with? Write a story about how you would be with someone if your life were a clean slate, and you didn't remember your past or his or hers. Better yet, be that way with him or her for a day or an evening.

- Ask your daughter, husband, friend, lover, questions that you think you already know the answers to. Listen to that person with the same attention you would give to someone you just met.

3. Sometimes we only look at something in a new light when we can't be the way we always were. The Hanged Man in the tarot deck hangs upside down by his foot from the Tree of Life. There is a ring of light around his head, an illumination of sorts. He is forced to look at life "upside down," from a new perspective. Some people think the Hanged Man is an ominous card. It is not. The man is not hanging by his neck. It is his foot that is snared by

a rope in the tree, which is, by the way, abloom with green leaves. He has to stop and surrender to something larger than himself.

A friend broke her ankle. After hobbling around for a few weeks, she began to see walking in a new and magical way. On vacation with her husband in California, her ankle still in a cast, driving down Malibu Beach, she impulsively rolled down the car window and yelled out to a rollerblader speeding down the boardwalk, "You don't know how lucky you are!"

"I just couldn't help it," she said. "To be able to skate seemed like such a miracle. He probably has no idea what it was all about, but I felt better."

When have you been forced to change your habits? How did that change your way of relating to your old, familiar world?

4. Take an ordinary object—a towel, a vase, a lawn chair, the steering wheel of your car. Really look at it. Use it as the basis for a story. Make something up.

Woman Who Dances with the Wind

"You're going to the Medicine Woman Retreat, aren't you?" It was Jan Sabraski on the phone. I hadn't talked to her in more than a year, but she's the kind of friend who just picks up wherever we left off, no matter how long it's been. I feel completely comfortable with her. "Dorothy Starlite, you know, that retreat in Wisconsin. It's in two weeks."

Three years ago I took a group of women to the Colorado Rockies for a wilderness retreat called "Voices and Visions:

Speaking Your Life, Living Your Vision." At the end of the week, we planned a sweat lodge. I was given Dorothy's name and she agreed to come and lead our sweat. A delightful middle-aged woman with dancing brown eyes and a ready smile, Dorothy left a lucrative job, training advertising executives, to follow a calling she couldn't quite articulate but could no longer ignore. She was to teach, but she didn't know how or what. For a year after she left corporate America, she lived in a tree house on her friend's land in Colorado. She no sooner established herself in her lofty home than a Native American medicine man paid her an unexpected visit. "I think there is someone here I am supposed to teach," he said.

She studied with him and others, traveling the country conducting sweat lodges, doing medicine card readings, and putting on medicine wheel workshops. By the time she founded the Sisterhood of the Medicine Heart a couple of years later, she understood that her work is to return the feminine consciousness to a yearning, dying earth. Although she has a phone number in Colorado, her home is her old white Plymouth Reliant. "You'd be surprised how much she holds," says Dorothy. "Everything I need, including five pillows. I never sleep in her though. I sleep around." Her eyes twinkle as she thinks of hospitable friends and strangers she meets on her travels who share their homes with her.

When Dorothy came to my salon last year on her way through Minnesota and offered to do readings for my clients, Jan had requested one. Dorothy showed Jan that an insurance agent can be a medicine woman, too. Or perhaps it is the other way around. The medicine woman sells insurance for a living, goes into management, and brings the feminine consciousness into the workplace. "I trained my own manager how to work with women," Jan said. "I was the first woman agent he had worked with. He was quite receptive. In fact, when I sold you that homeowner's policy, and you and he and I went out to lunch, he was surprised that the two of us sat together, leaving him to sit by himself on the other side of the booth. He said two men would never sit together like that without elbowing each other and teasing, or being very businesslike. He was impressed with the familiar ease we had with one another."

Jan didn't think of herself as a medicine woman then. When we first knew each other, I didn't think of myself that way either, yet I knew I had gifts to bring, insights to share. I remember getting a numerology reading one time. I have a number 33. I don't know much about numerology, but apparently this is a powerful number. The numerologist typed up the high points of the reading for me. The line I remember most clearly is "You are destined to become a teacher, touching many people's lives, somewhat on the order of Jesus Christ. Or you could do very well in real estate." I still laugh about that, but it occurred to me that maybe I have a lot more to contribute than I'd been willing to be responsible for. Jesus Christ—hard to relate to. Medicine woman—maybe.

The Medicine Woman retreat was designed to remind us of our power as healers and visionaries, seers and wise ones; it was a place for us to meet ourselves in our fierce, fiery feminine beauty. Mostly, as women, we don't think of ourselves that way, or if we do for a moment or a day or in a dream, we have no way to sustain the tension, nowhere to ride the energy. We second-guess our vision, we question our wisdom, and our beauty eludes us as, daily, we confront images of women that conform to a confining cultural standard. Our medicine is strong. Coming together we draw open the long neglected medicine pouches of our lives and see what is in there.

An important part of Dorothy's retreat was to find our medicine names. I have to tell you that I didn't just go into this all gung ho, with my sleeves rolled up. My mainstream mind chattered constantly: "What's all this weird stuff anyway? I'm too old for this. Medicine name. Right. I'm going to go home with some outdoor kind of thing, or probably some bird thing. How do I explain that? My name is Lynn, okay?"

But there is another side of me that is deeply aware of and connected to the non-linear, the points in time and space that merge me with other realities, that trusts the synchronicity of things, that knows I will be led to what I need; there is the side that is willing to quit listening to the chatter of my mind and listen, instead, to the murmur of my heart. Over time I have become willing to receive information in whatever form it comes, testing it against the map of my life, keeping what rings true and not bothering with the rest.

A few years ago when I was in Sedona, Arizona, I met a man who did Jeep tours to the energy centers in that area called vortexes. When I signed up, I thought we would drive around for an hour, he would point out the different vortexes, and I would go home and say, "Yup, I saw the Sedona vortexes."

But that's not what happened. At eight o'clock one morning, I piled into a Jeep with Paul, whom I had only met briefly the day before, and rode out to a godforsaken place in the red rocks of the high desert. Just he and I. As we breezed along a deserted highway in the early morning light, I thought, "What am I doing all by myself in this strange place with a man I hardly know?" We got out of the Jeep and hiked far into the hills until we came to a medicine wheel made of stones. "Let's sit here," he said. I sat.

We passed some time in silence before Paul spoke: "If you listen, the spirits of the earth speak." He began to carry on a conversation with the wind. As he talked, I joined in, as I might in any parlor conversation. I had been especially busy with my business at the time and struggling with a dying relationship. I was depleted. I had come to Sedona on a solo journey to rest and replenish.

"I want the wind to carry me like a bird in flight," I said. "I am so heavy and so tired. I ache to feel myself fly again!"

"You are not bird," said Paul, "nor are you wind. You are tree. You are ancient and wise, full of vision and strength. You need fly nowhere, for like tree, all you need comes to you. The sun warms you. The rain waters you. Flowers grow around you. Birds use your branches for home. Children play in your shade. The wind brings you notice of all that takes place on the earth. You protect and nourish. You are protected and nourished. If there is someone in your branches who weighs them down, that person must light elsewhere. You need go nowhere, but trust that all will be drawn to you. Meditate on tree. Talk to trees."

I have done that quite a lot since then, and I am learning in the midst of the hurry of my life to stop and listen, to talk to trees, and to remember my "tree-ness." Shortly after returning from Sedona, I found a wonderful painting by the artist Kiki of a laughing woman in a red dress, standing on a green hill, the yellow sun shining down on one side, blue raindrops watering her other side, many-colored flowers blooming around her feet. Her feet are roots and her upraised arms are branches. Underneath, in handwriting, is the inscription: I want to live as if I were a tree.

I bought the painting and hung it. I love it and I look at it often. It was made for me, I am sure. I have trouble with one thing about trees, though. They can't dance. Being so majestically rooted, they are leaden footed. My feet fly whenever they have the chance, to drums, Gershwin, or rock and roll. It doesn't matter. When my body doesn't dance, it goes dead. I go dead.

At Dorothy's retreat, I took my journal out to the woods where, earlier, Jan and I had met four grandfather oaks, baronial in stature, one of them gnarled and knotted, all their thick branches reaching up and out in magnificent gestures of praise. I had an hour before dinner to sit in their presence, listen to the silence, and write or think or dream as I pleased. Every time I heard an acorn drop, I thought it was a footstep, but there was no one but me and the trees.

I meandered through my journal, writing about the weekend, grappling with this idea of a medicine name.

"We are seeking our medicine names. I want to know mine and I think it is stupid. Other people here have been given their names in dreams. I'm afraid I am less receptive. Dense, maybe, like the woods. Road. Woods. I am here. I think, 'Oh, a bunch of middle-class women doing pointless exercises.' Then, I know the power of the feminine consciousness, rising, speaking, loving with open, healed hearts. This is my work."

I thought about names. I thought about how I am like the man from the Dagara tribe in West Africa whose name was given to him before birth. His name, Malidoma[1], which means "to be friends with the stranger/enemy," was his

---

[1] Malidoma Somé, *Of Water and the Spirit: Ritual, Magic, and Initiation in the Life of an African Shaman* (New York: G.P. Putnam's Sons, 1991)

destiny. As the western world began to encroach on his culture and erode its spiritual linkage to the earth, to the community, and to life itself, the elders decided he was to serve as a bridge between his culture and ours. He was to befriend the stranger/enemy. He was to go into the "wilderness" of modern civilization and share his experience, his knowledge and his love. He was to listen and teach.

But it was his name I was thinking of as I sat quietly in the woods with my journal. I often work in corporate settings, training people in stress management. Business, for me is not a heart place. It is like a desert, where people struggle for their lives in the face of productivity quotas and long hours. In many cases, it is a place that respects no rhythm but the tick of the clock, the ring of the register. I love the people I meet in the workplace. They are bright, articulate, and full of life, but as much as I try to like business and its trappings, I don't. Yet I stay in business settings to create a climate of well-being. The Conscious Body is the name of my company. That name came in a dream—it said when we take time to listen to our bodies, we begin to hear again the whisper of our hearts, the deep longing of our souls. I wondered if my name was Bridge Between Worlds. I wrote that down.

Other names came to me. Pathfinder, maybe. Reflection

on Still Water? A bird called when I wrote that one down. Then it was quiet again except for the sounds of wind in the trees and a cow mooing in the distance. I wrote:

The trees know where they are. The trees are not lost. Everything is a symbol and it is not. It is what it is. We make our meaning, don't we? We make sacred. Keep writing. Keep listening. Tell the truth.

It was time for supper. I rose quickly and headed up the path toward the camp dining room. It was quite a walk to the lodge and I was already late. I had gone several hundred feet when suddenly I did an about-face and headed for the grandfather trees I had sat near all afternoon. I had to talk to them. Don't ask me how I knew that. I just did.

I stood before them in the silence. They stood before me, four gracious hosts, wise diplomats. The wind lightly danced through their branches. Their branches danced with the wind. "Woman Who Dances with the Wind," they said. "Trees do dance. They dance with the wind. You are Woman Who Dances with the Wind."

It was done. I had my name. It will reveal its substance as I wear it, like a good shoe or a fine jewel.

Woman Who Dances with the Wind

Finding Your Stories

1. What's in a name? Names carry stories. Dive deep into the wealth of naming things and being named. Look here for story ideas:

   - Naming an animal (My brother's first son and his long-dead hunting dog have the same name. Coincidence?)
   - Naming a baby
   - How you got your name
   - Nicknames
   - The name of a town
   - The name of your secret club when you were ten
   - The name of your book club, business, etc. (One of my classes named themselves Women in Heat! A client has spent twelve years meeting with her Stitch and Bitch group. Great stories there.)
   - Names bestowed or found or lived into

2. There are stories within stories. Knowing where to pare is a good skill. Then you can take what you left out and make another story, if you want. For instance, not included in the "Giving Blanket" story in this book is the fact that Paul Thompson's grandmother, Elva, made the quilt he used for the giving blanket. The eleventh child of Swedish parents, Elva means eleven in Swedish. It would be intriguing to find out more and tell a story about how Elva fared with her name or why her mother and father gave her a number.

The Dog Leash
and Divine Order

I t was early May when my phone rang at the salon. The voice on the other end was not a client as I had expected, but someone from Philadelphia whom I had never met.

"Hi. This is Katherine Morris," the voice on the line said. "I'm going to be in Minneapolis for a midwives' convention next week. I got your name from the Earthstewards' resource list and wondered if we might be able to connect while I'm in town."

Earthstewards is an environmental organization that has

members all over the world. In the tradition of the early Essenes who opened their homes to travelers, Earthstewards asks that members across the globe get in touch as they travel. Katherine didn't need a place to stay, but she did want to rent a bicycle, explore Minneapolis, and perhaps spend a little time with me if she could. We made a date to walk around Lake Harriet Wednesday evening of the next week.

May in Minneapolis is exquisite. With my dog Mitzi in the back seat of my old Plymouth, I picked Katherine up at the front door of the downtown Hyatt. The last few days had been sunny and warm. Katherine had spent them skipping her conference and pedaling about the city, delighting in the fragrance of lilacs, the soft greens of the newly budding trees, the quaint bookstores, and the inviting neighborhoods.

"I thought this would be the trip from hell," she told me as we walked the three miles around the lake. Mitzi sniffed trees and strained at her leash. "Minneapolis is just not one of those places you hope to go. Too far north. Tundra. I'm here because it was my turn to represent our clinic at the national midwives' convention, so I had to come. But this is a beautiful place, more beautiful than I had ever dreamed. It is a sacred place."

We walked and talked, bathing ourselves in the breezes

blowing in off the lake. We came to a fishing dock and decided to stop there awhile to watch graceful sailboats glide across the water as the sun set. We sat in silence for some time.

Not so content as Katherine and I to sit still in the descending dusk, Mitzi shifted her position many times, lying down and sitting up, lying down and sitting up. Her chain leash caught between the planking of the dock. The links of the chain had twisted just enough so that I couldn't get them out, no matter how hard I tried.

I pulled. I pushed. I jiggled. I lifted. I twisted. I dug between the planking with my car key. I could not budge the chain.

"Divine Order," Katherine said.

"What?" I said.

"Divine Order. Say it. Divine Order. See what happens."

"Divine Order," I said, feeling rather foolish.

The chain lifted right out of the dock with no effort.

Katherine told me a story about how, after a long and fruitless search for an apartment in an overcrowded city, she whispered, "Divine Order," and found a charming apartment that very day. I listened and nodded, all the while thinking, "Just a fluke. Humor the woman." As she finished her story, Mitzi's chain got caught between the planks of the dock again.

I forgot all about Divine Order. I pulled, pushed, lifted, twisted, and turned. I dug with my car key. The leash did not budge.

"Just say, 'Divine Order'," nudged Katherine gently.

"Oh, all right. Divine Order!" I spat. This was really stupid, and I was getting riled.

The chain released immediately. I sat looking at it in my hand while Mitzi wagged her white tail, anxious to get moving again.

The fragrance of lilacs hung in the night air as we walked back to the car in the dark. I delivered Katherine to the Hyatt and returned home, Mitzi in the backseat, my life having been altered by a recalcitrant dog leash and a woman I have never seen or heard from again.

Divine Order.

The Dog Leash and Divine Order

Finding Your Stories

1. Anything can alter your life if you are receptive. I was listening to public radio the other day. A blues singer with a lifelong drug habit was talking about the last of his many stints in rehab. Every time in the hospital, he attended all the sessions, went through all the programs. Nothing had ever made a difference. He figured nothing ever would.

   One evening, a nurse handed the man an orange. Taking the orange, he saw his life in a new way. He knew in that moment he could quit drugs, and he did. He's been sober ever since. Was it the orange? Was it the nurse's kind gesture? Was the man simply ready to see a new possibility? He doesn't know. He just remembers the gift of an orange turned his life around.

   Today, allow someone to give you a gift that turns your life around.

2. List five examples of divine order in your life.

3. List five ways you close yourself off to divine order in your life.

4. Tell a friend a story about a coincidence that turned out to be especially fortuitous.

5. Ask friends to tell you about a chance meeting that changed them in some way.

6. Make a collage. Don't think about it. Don't plan it. Allow divine order to guide you. See what the images say to you.

III
Crafting Your Stories

I am going to say very little about craft.

Of course, learning to craft a story so that it vibrates with life is important. Good crafting pulls focus, creates movement, evokes feeling, raises questions, begs resolution. But without a firm footing in your own life—where you open to your stories—and without trust in your own way of seeing the world, the ability to craft a story is a moot point. You may have a lovely shell, but nothing alive makes its home within.

Being neither a performance storyteller nor a fiction writer, but someone whose purpose it is to help people articulate the stories that satisfy their souls, I focus more on going along to mine for gold than on polishing the ring to be made from it. I provide basic guidance in the craft department, but with the renaissance of storytelling all over the world, there are many, many resources available for polishing your craft if you want to keep going.

Oral storytellers emphasize the telling part. Many never write their stories at all. Others write first, then translate the written story into a told tale. There is a difference in feel between the written and the oral telling. Others use only the written word as a vehicle for the stories they tell. Yet others tell stories through song or dance, drawing or painting. I met a man in Santa Fe whose black pottery told his tribe's rich story. For an enchanting few minutes, I sat across from him on a blanket on the sidewalk bordering Santa Fe Plaza, moved by his presence, awed by the beauty of his pottery, enveloped by his story.

Every art generates teachers of its craft. You can find role models, books, tapes, workshops, degree programs, websites, and more. This is where the coach in me kicks in. I hold you as creative, resourceful, and whole and invite you to find ways to learn your craft that make you want to jump out of bed in the morning.

Here's what I will offer you: one great resource that will open you to a whole world of storytelling resources. It is:

The National Storytelling Network
101 Courthouse Square
Jonesborough, TN 37659
1-800-525-4514 or 423-913-8201
Fax: 423-753-9331
E-Mail: nsn@naxs.net
Website: www.storynet.org

The website includes a mind-boggling list of links that include bookstores, collections of stories, classes, regional organizations, and much more.

Just remember, though, if you focus up front on crafting your stories, you will squelch your natural playfulness and spontaneity. Playfulness begets creativity. You get down to the stuff of a good story by not censoring, judging, or trying to mold it too soon into a neat package. Nancy Mellon, author of *Storytelling & the Art of Imagination* (Element, Inc., Rockport, MA, 1992), remarks: "Our rational mind can sometimes interfere horribly with the actual essence of the story. There's something precious about the story that comes from the deep self. Often the story that gets rejected the most vehemently as an inferior creation is the one that carries the most important message."[1]

Another storyteller, Michael Burnham, shares his experience: "I got into a rut where I kept censoring and editing my favorite [stories], trying to make them perfect. But when I succeeded, they died." A technique he recommends to remedy editorial overkill is visualization, a type of rehearsal where you picture how the events of the story unfold as well as imagine yourself actually telling the story. This kind of right-brain activity frees up the teller in you to "show" the images as they flow.[2]

That being said, I will now give you a few guidelines I feel are essential to the craft of storytelling:

- If you don't feel compelled by a story, leave it alone. A good story can't wait to be told.

---

[1]Anne Cushman, "Once Upon a Time . . . " *Yoga Journal,* July/Aug. 1993: 103.

[2]Sam A. Marshall, "Storytelling: Dressing Up Your Words," *Toastmaster,* Jan. 1986: 9.

- A memorable story transforms in some way. Although it may recount an everyday situation, it has a universality that speaks to the human spirit.

- Establish a point of view. Are you telling your story from a child's point of view? A parent's? The next door neighbor's? The dog's?

- Create a setting. Describe where the story takes place using sensory images of sight, sound, smell, touch, taste.

- Show, don't tell. Let the characters unfold. In other words, instead of telling us "Michael's grandma was quirky," show us a word picture. "When Grandma Mildred visited Michael on Sundays, she always wore tap shoes and a feather in her hat" shows us what she's like.

- Include a beginning, a middle, and an end. If you have ever endured the torment of listening to a story without these essential elements, you will not want to inflict this fate on others. Think about the last time you listened to Uncle Leo drone on about his appendectomy.

- Raise a question that introduces some kind of conflict or tension at the beginning.

- Develop action in the middle. What happens? What actions do the characters take? How does the conflict escalate? This is the plot.
- Bring about some kind of resolution at the end.

Now, go back to playing. Play with these guidelines. Enjoy your mistakes as well as your triumphs. Tell, tell, tell to anyone who will listen. Watch their responses and listen to yourself as you do. Ask for constructive feedback. Get your ego out of the way as you hone your stories in the sharing.

I play with my writing, usually trusting that something will come out. I don't worry too much about what comes at first; I just let it come. In the process of writing this book, these stories have been edited twice. I am rarely married to my words. I see storymaking as a collaboration in many ways—between teller and audience, between teller and other tellers who listen for effective wording, timing, length, delivery, content, between writer and editor. Some of these stories I tell orally, others remain on the page as is.

I have been a writer for many years. And a poet. And a storyteller. Over the years, I have learned to see craft as a vehicle for revealing the essence of the piece. A well-crafted story draws attention to its essence not its mechanics.

On the other hand, one of my biggest lessons about creativity came out of working with the mechanics of meter and rhyme. One time, in a class, I started out writing a poem with a message I wanted to convey, but because I had chosen to craft it using iambic pentameter, I soon had to let the form take me where it would. I could not find words that fit my notion that would also fit the form. Finally, I surrendered to the form, and I crafted a new poem that surprised and delighted me. I loved it and would never have gone there had I not given the form permission to take me deeper. So there is a paradox here. Don't worry about form at first, but when you do start working with it, let it teach you. The true meaning of surrender is not to "give up," but to "give oneself over to." When you are ready, giving yourself over to your craft can help you tap deeply into your creative flow.

The stories that follow represent various aspects of story crafting. "The Giving Blanket," in being chosen runner-up in the 1997 National League of American Pen Women's Soul Making Literary Contest, was recognized for both craft and content. It was an honor to go to San Francisco and read an excerpt at the awards ceremony. "Listen Like the Deaf Man" lends itself well to telling because of its brevity and visual imagery. While people listen, I invite them to choose a stone of their own from one of the twig baskets I pass around the room. "Just Dorothy" uses the technique of repetition, which fits in with the repetitive nature of the questions someone with Alzheimer's disease asks. "The Goin' Home Bitterroot Blues" incorporates elements of a style of writing called "new journalism." Although the next story, "My Legs Are Fine, the Boots Don't Fit," is about the same trip to the mountains as "Bitterroot Blues," I chose to craft it as a separate story with its own distinct perspective. "Sit in a Chair" and "The Basketball Goddess" both reflect craft decisions that were intended to mirror the personalities of the people they are about, while at the same time reflecting values that are my own. "Zen and the Art of Toilet Paper" is another one I love to tell. I use the late Katagiri Roshi's Japanese accent and hand gestures to emphasize his way of being, and when I tell it, I leave off the last line.

The Giving Blanket

To get to Paul Thompson's forty-sixth birthday party, you had to park at the top of the hill and walk the half-mile down to the cabin with your potluck entree, your gifts, your overnight case, and your sleeping bag. But once you got there, it was like being in your own little paradise thirty short miles from home. The cabin, nestled into a bluff with its hand-hewn deck overlooking the St. Croix River, had been in Paul's family for years, and this is where he loved to be.

My partner, Bill (now my husband), went to the party with me. Bill knows Paul through me, but I've known Paul since my children were little. We've worked together in community development projects; I've cut Paul's hair; Paul worked for me for a while as a massage therapist; and we took an intensive six-month leadership training course together. The invitation got me thinking about my long and enduring friendship with Paul, and I really wanted to be part of his birthday celebration. We were asked to bring two gifts: something to share with Paul reflecting who he is for us and something to give away on the giving blanket.

Well, I could think of a lot of things to say about Paul, things I wanted to share with him and the other good friends who would be there. But I wasn't so sure what the giving blanket was all about. It said on the invitation to bring something you loved to place as a gift on the giving blanket.

The week of the party I had a million things to do, so when Saturday came and I hadn't decided what to bring for the giving blanket, I was in a minor panic. Something I love. Something that means a lot to me. Something that is a part of me. What? What should I bring? The dream catcher given to me as a gift? No. I couldn't part with that. The papier-mache box in the shape of a radiating golden sun? No. I hadn't had that long enough to make it mine. If it wasn't mine yet, how could I give it away? The book of goddess stories that tells about Huitaca, the bringer of perfume and play, touching and love? When the people of the village lived close to Huitaca, they lived with feeling under their skins. No. The gift of that story is in the telling. A book seemed too easy.

As I was rummaging through my things, a little talisman that I had made, a small cloth bundle of rainbow pink hues, tied at the top and hung from a hot pink silk cord, caught my eye several times. I had made it at one of the creativity retreats I conduct, a medicine bag to place around my neck for clarity and power in my creative endeavors. The little pouch contained soft, rose-colored petals, much like the petals a woman in our group had written a poem about making love in. They were to remind me to enjoy the sensual pleasures. It contained shards of blue birdshell to remind me of the delicacy of life, the tiniest pine cone you can imagine to represent growth, and a small stone to keep me grounded.

But the talisman really wasn't worth anything. The top of the cloth bag was frayed a bit, and who would understand about the stuff inside? Could something like this really be considered a gift? I thought maybe I was just too stingy to give something away I had bought. But giving the talisman was like giving a part of myself, something close to my heart, something that had meaning for me, and that is what I brought.

The gathering on the deck grew as night fell and the stars came out. The table inside groaned under the black beans, hijiki rice rolls, spinach lasagna, bean and cheese enchilada casserole, and good bread. I was in culinary heaven, but Bill is much more McDonald's than macrobiotic, so he brought a two-pound bag of M&M Peanuts to balance things out. I was glad. You have to have a little chocolate for good measure, as far as I'm concerned.

We ate out on the deck amid conversations about teaching school (Paul had just gone back into teaching fifth grade in an inner-city school after many years as a community organizer), the river traffic in the thirties, the love that went into building the cabin, and the long-ago summer spent there with Claudia, Paul's former lover, whose birthday is the same day as his, and who helped plan the party. Of the people there, I knew a few almost as long as I've known Paul. Others were recent additions to his large, ever-expanding circle of friends, including three teachers from his school and a woman who had answered a personal ad that Paul placed but who had decided, for whatever reasons, that he made a better friend than a date.

After dinner, we lit candles all around the deck, and Claudia and Paul unfurled a blue blanket on the floor in our midst. "We are going to start the giving ceremony now," announced Paul. "If you've never done this before, this is how it works. Everyone brings their gift to the circle. Before laying it on the blanket, tell us what it is and why you brought it. There is a gift here for everyone, and each person will know which gift is theirs. The gift is in the giving, the passing along of something we have loved, and in the receiving of something given freely, of something we may not have even known was ours."

I enjoy ceremonies like this, especially among friends, but Bill is a little more skeptical. He has less tolerance for the intangible, and a tendency to be more linear. He says he's not very spiritual, but what I see is a man of heart who fights all the time with a culture of the head. He spends hours picking out wrapping paper and ribbons to design beautiful packages that contain thoughtful birthday, Christmas, or just-a-surprise-for-you gifts. I admired his plunge-right-in spirit as he sat in the circle with everyone, having brought a small bottle of massage oil to provide whoever took it with the touch, pleasure, and relaxation we enjoy when we give each other massages.

One by one, the gifts were laid on the blanket. A woman began, "This glass frog was given to me by my father when I was a little girl. It meant a lot to me. It still does, but in my heart I know it is time to pass it on. With it I pass on my father's spirit and his love." "This is a book I have loved and read over and over again," explained another woman. "It contains wisdom and laughter that touches me. May it touch you now." "Some squash and red peppers from our garden," offered a man. "Food from the good earth grown with love." "I like to think I'm an artist," ventured another man. "I draw late at night when it is quiet and I have done my lesson plans for the next day." He slid a charcoal drawing of an Indian's strong face, which looked a lot like his own face, from a manila envelope and showed it to us. He placed the picture on the blanket. I waited until almost the end, told the story of the talisman pouch, and lay it on one of the few bare spots remaining on the overflowing blanket.

As I sat there watching the gifts gather, listening to people give little parts of their lives in the form of a frog or a book or a tomato or a charcoal drawing, thinking that I am to take something in the end, I felt uncomfortable. I was giving something that had no monetary value. I was to take something I wanted. As the stars sprinkled the sky, voices rose and fell and bodies got up and sat down, the blanket filled with objects. I thought about value. I thought about giving and taking. I felt shame about not giving enough. I felt shame about wanting. What if someone else wanted what I want? What if there is a run at the blanket? I will just sit and wait, I thought. I'll watch and see. What if no one takes my gift?

After the last person spoke and placed his gift on the blanket, Paul asked us all to take a moment of silence in gratitude for each other and the fullness of our lives, for abundance and sharing. Then he said, "Come and choose your gift."

People stepped up to the blanket one at a time, or sometimes from different sides two or three at a time, each taking something that had caught their eye. Several things interested me, but the drawing of the Indian called to me as if it had a voice. Here was the creative process in action, just the thing I had been preoccupied with myself as I was writing my first book, hiding the stories in an envelope. Here in this picture was the creation of art in the midst of a life that demands a full workday and a view of ourselves as "not artist" or "trying to be artist." The shadowed face with the high cheekbones and the wise eyes was a powerful presence brought alive by the hand of the artist. I rose and took the gift back to my seat.

The blanket now was almost empty. The pink pouch glared at me from the blue expanse. I knew it. It was a silly thing to bring. I didn't explain it well enough. It had no practical value. Then, from the chair beside me, Bill quietly walked over to the blanket and picked up the talisman. Bill? Bill doesn't have any interest in such things. He never scoffs at my interest, but he likes useful things like kitchen utensils or shoe horns or clothing or tools, or fun things like the plastic M&M Peanut machine that dispenses M&M Peanuts when you pull its arm, or the yellow, blue, and red Dairy Queen watches, of which he bought five because he wanted to have one always. Bill? And at that moment I felt completely loved, but didn't know why until later.

After the giving blanket ceremony ended, people needed a stretch and ice cream and birthday cake to sustain them for the dancing later on. A gregarious group, they shared stories and songs and comedy performances on the deck. Later we danced to the Stones, the Dead, Mickey Hart's *Planet Drum,* klesmer band tapes, Sweet Honey in the Rock, and all kinds of rock, rhythm, blues, and funk—no partners in particular but a free-for-all, move-as-the-music-moves-you kind of thing. The night wind kept us cool under the blue-black sky until it grew very late. Several people were staying overnight, sharing the available floor space inside the cabin. Bill and I decided to go to bed up in the loft where we had staked out a mattress earlier in the evening. We fell into a deep sleep and awoke in the morning refreshed.

Something about the river air made us all a little laid back and content. Claudia had set out muffins and toast, yogurt and granola, coffee and juice. Partake if you wish, eat what you please. Bill and I took a walk down the beach, later joined a conversation on the deck, did a few dishes, and prepared to leave. We gathered our things for the walk up the hill.

It wasn't until we were in bed the next night that I understood what had happened when Bill took my gift from the giving blanket at Paul's party. In the taking, it was Bill who gave the gift, one I had hungered for all my life. By taking the talisman, he said to me, "I value this part of you. I value the gifts you bring. Even though I don't understand it completely, I am open to it. I am open to you." He allowed me to contribute something of my deepest self to him and he saw me as I am.

It was one of those you-know-it-when-you-feel-it kind of things. Ah ha. This is the kind of love I had craved when I was a little girl—so simple, so observant, so embracing, so generous, so kind. The woman I am now can receive it. In the wash of this realization, I just held Bill until I could speak. "Thank you for your gift," I said. "It surprised me that you took my pouch. It touched me beyond words." He stroked my forehead, holding me, rocking me. "I am here," he said. "I am here."

The Giving Blanket

Finding Your Stories

1. Knowing we are loved is like coming home. Tell a story in which a gesture or a word opens the floodgates of love.

2. Tell a story about a birthday party.

3. Is giving easier for you than receiving? Or do you like to get and not give? Are you ambivalent about both? What have you been given that you treasure? What should you give away that you haven't? Make up a tale about giving and receiving, or tell one from your life.

4. Think of a friend you've had for many years. Don't just describe the friend, but tell a story that reveals what that person is like.

Listen Like the Deaf Man

A s owner of one of the earth-friendly businesses participating in the Green Expo at the Mall of America, I felt out of place and overwhelmed. Yes, the vision fit. I had dedicated my salon, The Conscious Body, a Center for Hair, Body, and Being, to the enhancement of personal, community, and global well-being. The salon carried earth-friendly products and, through their use, educated clients about the environment.

Through a home-based studio, I, along with a team of other professionals, did hair care and therapeutic massage, and offered on-site neck and shoulder massage to the corporate world. I developed classes and seminars on stress management, creativity, and healthy body image. Through my work with the whole person, I have observed that understanding our bodies, their cycles, and their needs makes it possible to understand more fully and respond to the greater body we all share—the earth, its cycles, and its needs.

By deliberately choosing to stay small, I was able to know each client The Conscious Body served and respond personally to him or her. I tended to stay clear of places like the Mall of America, the largest shopping center in the world.

When you have a booth at an expo like this, it is customary to give away some kind of a premium, along with your literature, that reminds people of who you are and what you do. I thought for quite some time about what to give away. I could give away recycled writing tablets bearing The Conscious Body logo. I could give away imprinted pens. I could give away key chains with little plastic globes attached. Nothing fit. What would people who had their arms full of stuff from the mega-mall do with more stuff? What could I give away that would make a difference to those who received it?

Business people say the question should be: What could you give away that would make people remember your business? In such a large place, get flashy. Play loud music. Show a video. But I don't seem to be wired up that way. At the time I was planning for this expo, I had been thinking about stones.

In the Native American tradition, stones carry the wisdom of the earth. They were here when the earth began. They have come up to the surface from the center. Stones, it is said, keep the earth's records. I had read a story by Annie Dillard, "Teaching a Stone to Talk," about a man who spent his life trying to teach stones to talk. Everyone laughed at him. The people of the town knew teaching a stone to talk was impossible, yet he kept on. It was a good story, but I got to thinking how a Native American would laugh at the premise of teaching a stone to talk. Stones speak already. It is we ourselves who must be taught to listen.

Soon, the idea of giving away a premium distilled into the simpler idea of giveaway. In the native tradition, you give away something just to give it away. It is a gift with no strings attached. What would make a difference to each person I came in contact with in the overstimulated rush of the mega-mall? Then it came to me. A stone, of course.

I called Douglas, the man who planted my lilac bushes two summers ago, and asked him where I could get enough plain river rock to give to mall shoppers who came by the booth. He brought me three huge buckets of small rocks. Their grays, reds, browns, and whites were encrusted with dirt and grass. For three days I had to use my downstairs shower because my upstairs bathtub was full of soaking stones.

At the booth, I set the washed stones out in twig baskets with a sign on the table saying, "Please select a stone." A small paper inspired by Native American author and teacher Jaimie Sams went with each stone. It read: "The earth is a conscious body. Stone is the tool and the teacher for returning to and learning from the earth. To quiet your mind and feel the deep balance of the earth, hold a stone in your hand. You will begin to breathe with the earth. Then listen. The ancient stones are the earth's record keepers. Connecting with stones can teach you every lesson about living in harmony with the earth."

People who are power shopping are on the move. They look past what is right in front of them to the next brightly lit window, the next gigantic sale. Even though there were thousands of people whizzing by the booth, they didn't stop. The first day I stood in the aisle with my basket of stones asking everyone, "Would you like a stone?" It was the only way I would get to talk to anyone.

I was promoting our corporate on-site massage services, but most of the people I talked to were from Ohio or Japan or Iowa. Everywhere but Minnesota. My market was local businesses, so this was not a fit at all. I still had two twelve-hour days left in this perfectly engineered world of indoor trees, diffused light, slick entertainment, fast food, white noise, and perpetual motion. I felt like I was trapped inside a space station far from the living earth the expo was intended to remind people of.

Some people stopped to talk to me out of curiosity. Some took a stone. Kids lit up. They had no trouble with the idea of listening to a stone. Adults, for the most part, were puzzled, but a few understood. One woman, after selecting her stone, remembered her childhood on the farm. The smell of the stone brought back memories of good earth there.

A handsome young man in a silk shirt and well-cut trousers came by my booth late in that first afternoon. Out of the corner of my eye I saw him bending over the basket of stones on the table. When I had finished talking to the person I was with, I turned to the young man to explain about the stones. He straightened up and signed to me that he was deaf.

I just stood next to him, then, as he returned to the stones. He picked one up, turned it slowly in his hands, and pressed it to his heart. The noise around me hushed. The activity seemed to cease. The profound silence surrounding this man allowed for deep listening right there in the middle of the mall. I remained there for some time as he picked up another stone, then another, listening to each the same way until one clearly spoke to him. His smile flashed recognition. This was his stone. "Thank you," he signed, and walked off, still smiling, into the crowd.

No. Thank you, I say to that man. I realized that he is why I came to the mall. I thought I was bringing something to people with my stones and maybe I did. But he brought the meaning of my message to life with his profound listening.

He taught me that listening is not something you do with your ears, but something you do with your heart. It is what you bring with your being, with your full presence. It does not need a special setting but can be generated even in the midst of chaos. He taught me that silence is not the absence of something but the wellspring of what is possible. It is the essence of deep ecology.

I have told this story over and over in corporation after corporation when I am speaking about stress management. While telling the story, I pass a basket of stones and ask each person to select one for themselves. At the end, I suggest that people keep their stone with them, in their pocket or at their desk. When life gets too full, when the phone is ringing, the projects just keep coming, when the boss is impossible or the children are sick at home, I ask this:

Hold your stone in your hand. Remember how old it is. Think of the millions of years it has been in existence and become aware of how your life fits into the bigger picture of all life on the planet. Quiet your mind and begin to breathe with the earth. Listen . . .

Listen to each other. Listen to the earth. Listen to your-self. Listen to your life.

Listen like the deaf man.

Listen Like the Deaf Man

Finding Your Stories

1. Spend some time with stones this week. Notice them. Pick them up. Often we only go for the pretty stones. See what different stones have to say to you. Become very quiet and let a stone tell you a story.

2. Find a stone that speaks to you. Keep it with you. When you are feeling overwhelmed or stressed, take a moment to look at your stone and hold it in your hand. Feel how old it is, how much older than you. Remember how long this stone has been here, and how much it has seen. Place your life in the context of this stone's life. Does this alter your perspective on the present situation? If so, how?

3. What does your stone tell you about living in harmony with the earth? With yourself? With other people?

Just Dorothy

I t was time to balance my mother's checkbook again. She lived on Blaisdell Avenue in an apartment, only a block away from my house. Her memory had begun to slip, quite gradually at first, but now it was hard for her to do many little tasks that had always come easily. I checked in on her almost every day.

On the short walk over to Mom's that day, the sun cloaked me in its warmth after a long, gray Minnesota winter. Robin song carried lightly through the branches of the budding elms. I took a deep breath, drinking in the sweetness, the freedom of the moment. I knew Mom's small apartment would be hot, and that as much as I wanted to help, it was not easy being with her. Our relationship had improved over the years, but even when she was well, we thought very differently. Our conversations aborted like so many liftoffs at Cape Canaveral, and I wanted to travel the galaxy with her.

We remained earthbound. Now with her impending Alzheimer's disease, it was like wearing lead shoes. "Are my checks all right?" "When do we pay taxes?" "I should invest in something different." "I can't invest in something different. The bank may fail." "Have I paid the rent?" "Are my checks all right?"

As usual, I piled the checks on Mom's table, got out the calculator, and started sorting. She sat on her beloved green French provincial couch, watching and waiting. As much as she tried to sit quietly, she couldn't help asking her questions. I would always answer briefly and as politely as I could, although I know my impatience came through as I scribbled things in and crossed things out. I wanted to concentrate on the numbers and finish the task at hand.

"Are my checks all right?" asked Mom tentatively.

Unlike all the other times, all the months and years before when I loved her but was driven crazy by her no matter how she was, that ordinary, repetitive moment opened between us like a flower as I glanced up from my work to answer her question. I looked into my mother's eyes and saw her face as if for the first time. She was not the Dorothy I thought I knew; not the person who asks tedious questions; not my mother who did or did not do all the things a mother should do; not a woman of eighty-four, someone with whom I don't see eye to eye. She was just Dorothy. And she was so beautiful.

There was no need at that moment to balance the checkbook.

"Mom, I want to thank you for all you have done for me," I heard myself say from the very core of my being. She had gotten up from her chair, but stopped short on her way to her tiny kitchen. Though partially blind, she looked directly at me.

"Lynn, I love you so much. I wish I could have done more."

"Mom, you gave me my life. What more could you have done?" I had been the blind one all these years and now I saw. There was nothing more to do.

She held out her hands to me. We sat down together on the green couch for the rest of the afternoon. She told me stories about growing up in St. Paul and about my father who had died when I was a child and about how she still missed him.

After that, nothing changed that you could see. Mom was still Mom, funny, stubborn, forgetful, and asking the same questions over and over. And I still got impatient with her sometimes. But in that one moment, everything had changed. In that one moment I knew who my mother was, and even as she became more frail and dependent in her illness, I was able to be with just Dorothy all the rest of her life. And she was so beautiful.

Just Dorothy

Finding Your Stories

1. When Yul Brynner was dying of cancer, I saw him interviewed on television. His wife was at home with him during part of the interview. He said the more he thought about his life, the more he realized that what other people bring is a gift, pure and simple. He had quit expecting things of his wife and began to receive with gratitude what she brought. He could be in her presence and be present with her. That is the space of love.

    Today, be with someone you love as if you had only a few more days to be with him or her. Do this for a full day. Share with that person what happened.

2. Like Alice tumbling down the rabbit hole to Wonderland, create a world that is unlike your own. An entrance pulls you in like a magnet and whoosh! There you are, looking around this preposterous, upside-down kind of place. Describe where you are and what you see. Wander about. Get your bearings. Encounter the

people and the beings that are there. Take in the colors, sights, and sounds. Take your time with this. Suddenly, a person you are so familiar with in your regular world strolls into view. What happens when you see this person? What do you say or do? What do they say to you? How do you feel? What part of this person do you see? In a world where everything is different, can you relate to this person in the same old way? Do you see something about this person that you don't see in your day-to-day life?

3. I've noticed that when people die, the things that drove me nuts about them when they were alive are the things that I remember with fondness or humor when they're gone. I've seen it happen with others as well. For instance, my friend Liz was particular about eating and serving fresh, whole foods. Her teenage sons complained loudly and often about the tofu and bean sprouts that were standard fare at their house. At Liz's funeral reception, her son David embellished stories about his experience with the meager selection of snack foods in the fridge—one avocado, three alfalfa sprouts and a slice of whole wheat bread—in a very funny way. Yup, that was Mom!

Suddenly, Mom's food habits were seen in a new light. When Liz and all she brought would not be there anymore, what was once annoying became an endearing memory. It's a shame to wait until someone we love is gone before we can fully appreciate them. Can you take an annoying habit of a loved one and reinterpret it like David did with the sprouts? Make it into a funny story.

The Goin' Home
Bitterroot Blues

Janet, the ride secretary, and her husband, Bob, pull into the driveway of the Princess Teakwitha Motel in Lewiston, Idaho, where I had spent the night. I toss my duffel bag into the back of their Ford pickup. Behind the truck, two Appaloosa horses ride calmly in a trailer. I slide onto the seat next to Janet. Bob is driving. Outside of Lewiston, we begin an immediate climb toward Musselshell encampment in the Bitterroot Mountains where the ride begins. To reach Musselshell, you leave Highway 12 at Greer,

Idaho, follow 12 from Greer to Weippe, and go straight east (on Pierce Street) for thirteen miles. Greyhound doesn't know where this is. I checked.

I have always loved horses. When I was little, I had imaginary cowboy friends, hundreds of them, a few with names who even took baths with me. After Annie Oakley had her own show on TV, I had a cowgirl friend too. Before that I didn't know I could invent a cowgirl. Dale Evans just didn't work for me. When the Sears catalog featured a cowgirl outfit, I wheedled my mother into ordering it for me, but I found it disappointing. It had a skirt, and you can't ride a horse in a skirt.

My dad started taking me to Shady Valley Riding Stable when I was seven. There he paid $1.75 an hour for me to sit on a horse named Jewel and wait for her to decide whether or not to walk. Then there was my ceramic horse collection stabled on a bookshelf in my bedroom, and later, when I was twelve, my parents bought me a real horse. I declared when I was in first grade that I would marry a cowboy and own a ranch when I grew up, and that's just what I did.

All my life I spent with horses. All my life, that is, until my horse trainer husband and I divorced nine years before the ride. The divorce left me shaken and bitter. In the name of a dream I had overextended myself, caring for thirty horses, a husband, and two baby daughters, while trying to maintain a full-time job and some semblance of personal autonomy. One evening after Dick and I had separated, but before we sold the land we had worked so hard for, I lay for comfort in the summer grass watching the sun splash purple over the western hills. I realized that in the seven years of our marriage I had not taken the time to lie in the grass and watch even one sunset. At that moment, horses became part of a past life, blamed for all I had missed, in my way like steamer trunks. From then on I would travel light with Samsonite, looking for the way back home.

But even though I moved to the city, I could not get rid of the horses. They paraded into my dreams, dropping, year in and year out, what a friend understood to be fertilizer. She waited until I was ready to listen before she mentioned this. "Horses are your special helpers," she suggested. "In their essence lies the ability to piece together the fragments of a broken spirit. Do you think you would ever like to have horses in your life again?"

"Of course not," I snapped. "That was in the past. Besides, how could it ever be?"

The next day I called Diane Hunz, a girl I used to ride

horses with in high school. Married now with three kids, she still owns horses. We talked about old times, our rides together, her marriage, my marriage, how much fun she had before anybody's marriage traveling out to the Bitterroot Mountains to go on a hundred-mile trail ride. "You know," she said wistfully, "the Appaloosa Association still sponsors that ride. I'd really like to go again."

As it turned out, Diane couldn't go that year. But as soon as I hung up the phone, I knew I was going. I had to.

This journey to the mountains took on the urgency of a she-bear searching for a lost cub. I am here despite a traveling companion backing out at the last minute, despite no substitute transportation (we were to use her car), despite not owning a horse. I am here after several desperate phone calls to the ride secretary at the National Appaloosa Association headquarters in Moscow, Idaho, reporting no luck with finding a ride with any of the names she supplied. "If you can get to Lewiston," she offers kindly, "Bob and I will come down from Moscow and pick you up on our way to Musselshell. The buses don't go there."

"I know," I said, relieved, knowing I will come up with money for a plane ticket to Lewiston if I have to pawn my mother's silver.

The hills are a dry brown. "No rain for quite some time," muses Bob. The creeks are running, though, and the rivers, the clear, deep water bubbling through the valleys; it's a sight to knock you off your saddle if you were sitting on top of a horse instead of inside a pickup. We chat about Janet's new white straw hat and Bob's battered brown one. "Maybe he'll lose it in a good wind," laughs Janet. "Can't go chasin' after it off the side of a mountain. He keeps findin' it every time I sneak it into the trash." Their two children are left at home in Moscow with Grandma, as are mine in Minneapolis. Janet and Bob seem to like each other a lot for people who have been married for thirteen years.

Driving along, they curse the fishing privileges granted the Indian residents of the area. "Those Indians think they can run the place," steams Janet. "What with tax-free goods available on the reservation, people go out there and buy cigarettes and things. Kinda cheats the rest of us out of our due."

My stomach knots. I wonder how these two can be so blind, these people who have put so much into arranging a ride commemorating part of the flight from the U.S. Cavalry of peace-loving Chief Joseph and his people.

For more than half a century, beginning in 1805 when members of the Lewis and Clark expedition were the first whites to meet them, the Nez Perce kept peace with the white people who settled in increasing numbers on their lands. A government report dated 1866 indicated what was to come: "This valley should be surveyed as soon as practicable, for the wigwam of the savage will soon give way to the whites. Instead of hunting and fishing grounds of the red man the valley will teem with a thriving and busy population." By 1877, dignified and eloquent Chief Joseph (also known as Hinmahtooyahlatkekht—Thunder Rolling in the Mountains) faced a hopeless and tragic confrontation. The Idaho government ordered the Nez Perce onto a reservation.

Chief Joseph responded this way:

All men were made by the same Great Spirit Chief. They are all brothers. The earth is the mother of all people, and all people should have equal rights upon it. You might as well expect the rivers to run backward as that any man who was born a free man should be contented penned up and denied liberty to go where he pleases . . .

Joseph, however, agreed to go to the reservation peacefully.

But on the way, three young warriors unleashed their bitterness, killing four settlers well-known as Indian haters. Joseph did not condone the violence, but, as guardian of his people, he stepped in to protect them. Joseph knew there would be no further talks with the government. What had happened would be seen as an act of war. General Howard would be after them all.

Chief Joseph and his 750 tribespeople, 500 of them women and children, fled. In the name of peace, they journeyed 1,700 miles, with 2,000 horses, through this wilderness, down the Bitterroot Valley, through Yellowstone, over the Montana plains seeking refuge in Canada with the exiled Sitting Bull. After a hard three and a half months, Joseph and 300 freezing, starving survivors were ambushed in a surprise attack by a Colonel Miles Nelson, leading 400 fresh troops. Many of Joseph's remaining people were killed, and he surrendered forty miles south of the Canadian border, all hope of returning to his beloved land, lost.

With these words, he surrendered:

It is cold and we have no blankets. The little children are freezing to death. My people, some of them, have run away to the hills, and have no blankets, no food. No one

*knows where they are—perhaps freezing to death. I want
to have some time to look for my children, and see how
many of them I can find. Maybe I shall find them among
the dead. Hear me, my chiefs! I am tired. My heart is sick
and sad. From where the sun now stands I will fight no
more forever."*

Bob navigates the shortcuts to Musselshell, the starting point for this year's 100-mile segment of the Chief Joseph ride that will take us through the Bitterroots' Lolo Pass and into Montana. We roll into the encampment before noon.

About a hundred tents are already set up in the vast clearing that was once a summer camping area for the Nez Perce, who bred sure-footed horses suited to the mountains. Explorer Merriweather Lewis noted that their large herds included "eligantly formed" [sic] horses "with large spots of white" on their hindquarters. He was describing the first Appaloosas. Near the tents today, about 250 horses with roughly a million spots sprinkled over their collective hindquarters stand tethered to whatever is available.

Sitting on a lawn chair behind the card table that serves as the ride secretary's office, I marvel at the stream of trucks and trailers bumping steadily into the grounds. License plates read New York, Texas, Tennessee, Colorado, Kentucky, Vancouver . . . I sample secretariness as I fill in for Janet.

A bewhiskered man with a paunch overhanging his silver belt buckle calls me Honey as he asks for some bit of information. Others like him drop in to see Janet, "the little secretary." The little secretary who planned all this and coordinated it even to the detail of picking me up at the Princess Teakwitha Motel. The little secretary who handles the paperwork, the nationwide publicity, and all manner of people.

I have pitched my tent behind Janet and Bob's truck. A nut-brown rig the size and shape of a Zephyr bus eases in next to me. On my other side is parked a pickup camper with two horses knotted to the attached trailer. I eye the distance between one of the spotted rear ends and my tent and decide to move my tent a little to the left. I wonder how I will get back to Minneapolis. Surely, of the 400 people who will arrive by the end of the day, someone could drive me back to Minneapolis after the ride. If I have to, I'll fly back, but I would rather catch a ride.

Betty Cowhick sashays over to the ride secretary's office all smiles. Like a proud child she unfurls an unfinished liquid embroidery wall hanging of a rearing Appaloosa stallion. At the end of the ride, she intends to donate her work of art to the national association. To emphasize her dedication to the art of liquid embroidery (and to the Chief Joseph Trail Ride), she models the design on the back of her green sweatshirt. Circular lettering commemorating a previous Chief Joseph Ride frames a standing Appaloosa gazing into some distant pasture. She executed the design herself using her extensive Liqui-Tex collection. As she twirls front, I glimpse a round patch, hand-sewn above each breast, one green and black "Ohio Sheriff's Posse" and one red, white, and blue "God Loves America." Betty's husband, Charlie, just bought six red-brimmed Chief Joseph adjustable caps for the folks back home from a man raising funds for his Kentucky Appaloosa club.

I wonder about these two, Betty especially. I am always fascinated by characters. Usually, against my conscious desires, I gravitate toward the unusual people, the funny ones, if you know what I mean. Even in high school, all I ever wanted was to fit in, to be included by the right people. But the right people were never very interesting, though I didn't realize it at the time, and it was a drag trying to get right for them, so I kept ending up with people like Barbara

Otts, the class misfit. Well, here I am on a very special journey, a pilgrimage if you will, and Betty Cowhick shows up. I resolve to stay as far away from her as possible. I withdraw to look for my rented horse.

Joe is tied to a red trailer. His tail is practically hairless, all but useless for swatting flies. He's a tall gangly gray with black spots peppering his rear end. I saddle him up, apprehensive about how we will get along, hoping he is not a funny horse. Really, I had pictured more of a beauty, a steed fitting for this soul journey. We trot up and down the road. He is a little apprehensive about me too. He moves well. I decide he will do.

The next morning I meet a handsome cowboy named Roger when he is stalled in the long line of vehicles on their way to be parked at our destination point. A bus will bring the drivers back so we can all ride out early tomorrow morning. Exiting a couple hundred trailer-pulling vehicles via one gravel road takes a long time, so Roger and I get acquainted. Roger is a clone of my ex-husband, whom I have not seen in the nine years since our divorce. "A rerun of my marriage?" I wonder. "No, I'll probably never see him again with all these people here, and just as well, too. I didn't come here for that, God forbid."

I ponder that day what I did come here for, and the urgency that brought me. I came here not knowing, open. If a broomtailed gray gelding and a rerun of my marriage are a part of it, perhaps, if I listen, I will hear my truth. Even Betty Cowhick, bless her heart . . . No, that's going too far. I'll leave Betty out of this.

The following morning at eight we ride out in mist, hundreds of horses and riders ready to tackle the hairpin, uphill trails. All day we climb. I look up and see horses single file above me. I look back and see horses single file below me. Horses and trees and trees and mountains and horses. The ride has begun. We put in a full day, watering thirsty animals in rushing spring-fed streams, resting occasionally under white pines, but climbing, climbing toward a sizzling steak dinner at our destination, twenty-one miles from Musselshell.

By evening everyone is pretty well settled. Although the day was hot enough for short sleeves and even bathing suit tops, the cool night air brings out sweaters and down vests. The pines seem taller than skyscrapers. You have to look straight up to see the moon. I am reminded of that dusk many years ago lying in my yard, watching the sun set over the purple hills, and I remember my resolution to take time. People are here, but time is too, for each of us—except for Janet, who is always busy.

Every night after supper, people mosey over to the portable dance floor to rock 'n' roll. Members of a country western band ride by day and make music by night. People crowd around a magnificent bonfire conversing, confabulating, philosophizing, pontificating, and just plain chewing the fat in idioms, drawls, dialects, twangs, and tweets, the likes of which converge in one spot rarely. Once a year these people come from all over to see each other.

Some, like Betty Cowhick, wear memento pins from the last five or six rides on their hatbands. Ninety-two-year-old Doc Johnson stands around the fire warming hearts with tales of the last fifteen rides. "That first year there were but forty cowhands up here in this wilderness," he reminisces. "I wouldn't miss coming here if I were on my deathbed." As he leaves to ask a young woman to dance, I remember how, earlier in the day, Doc did a galloping dismount ala the Cisco Kid, doctor kit in hand, to aid a woman who had been thrown from her horse.

I am standing around listening to all this, when I suddenly become aware of Roger breathing rather heavily near the back of my neck. "Dance?" he inquires. I love to dance, so I say yes. Roger dances the way some men do so that you spend about two-thirds of the time with your weight on one foot. Kind of mince stepppp, right leffftttt, mince stepppp, right leffftttt, in a small circle, cheek to cheek. I wonder if his right leg is as sore as my left. I learn as we dance that Roger's sun sign is the same as my ex-husband's. His German background is almost identical. His dark hair accentuates his blue eyes. Uncanny. His blue jeans, likewise, accentuate his cute buns. Deja vu. "All I want to do is raise horses," he drawls. "I'd describe myself as reserved but determined," he whispers into my ear. Uh huh.

Although Roger and I are first-timers on this annual ride, we are used to being on a horse. We enjoy the long days in the saddle under the hot sun as if the rhythm of our horses' hooves strikes the exact note of wonder that we came here to remember.

Everyone wasn't feeling as easy about it as we were, though. Hal, his new jeans crisp, his Harvard windbreaker a bit worn, is trying his hand at riding for the first time ever. Not even a lesson back in Seattle. His sister, Joan, has taken a whirl around a paddock once or twice. By the end of the second twenty-some-mile day, sitting down hurts. Bending over hurts, as does pitching a tent and bathing in the cold river, not to mention dancing. The band plays "Help Me Make It Through the Night." I lead Hal and Joan, hobbling, behind the cook tent where the generator pumps juice to the whining guitars. We practice a few yoga stretches. No one can hear their sad wails over the rumble-drone-rumble of the generator. Dancing comes a little easier after loosening up. We pass around a bottle of Gallo chablis blanc. Loosening up comes a little easier. Then sleep.

I lie in the bear grass thicker and softer than a stack of Hungry Jacks, listening. The moon and stars peep through the pines; I breathe the forest into my dreams. At dawn, one horse calls as if a blast of chill wind blows strong from between her ribs. From across the distance other horses whinny answers. We are all friends who sleep on the ground in the mountains, zipped in our down bags. We have all lain with the same fertile lover. The immense silence emits human morning sounds. A cough. A sneeze. A toothbrush rattling in a cup. An early riser catching breakfast before the line gets too long. We ride out at eight o'clock sharp, but right now, each of us will rise in our own due time.

I am inside the portable outhouse with the traditional half moon carved high on the door, the function of which, on this trip, is to thread your horse's lead rope through so you can hold on to him while you pee. I am in there and this thing happens where I get a sense of what it must have been like when people lived together in community, on the land, without the benefit of separation by wooden walls or barbed wire fences. I hear people laughing. I hear people arguing. I hear dishes clattering and horses pawing and birds chirping and daily business happening. For an instant, there in that outhouse, I exist outside of time and space. It is as if I know what being human is all about: No one is left out. We are all part of this thing, whether we are mad or glad, asleep or awake, willing or unwilling. Part of it whether we know it or not.

For the past four days, Roger and I have been trying to ride together. It doesn't work. Roger's horse, Snipper, likes to trot, even up mountains. My horse, Joe, likes to sightsee, leisurely like. We usually manage to meet for lunch. On the fourth day, I'm getting out my cheese sandwiches; Roger is hitching Snipper to a tree. "How ya doin', fella?" he says to his horse, giving him an affectionate pat. "You sure got a lot of energy. You and I, we sure are a pair, right, Snip? We'll take it easy for a while now, rest up, as if you needed it. Ha, ha, ha. Atta boy, fella." He and that horse had quite a conversation.

Roger has peanut butter and jelly. We sit under a tree, eating silently. Over the last four days, I have asked Roger about his life, his hopes, his dreams, his family. I have run out of things to ask. "Don't you want to know anything about me?" I finally venture.

"Oh, no. It'll all come out eventually," he shrugs.

Tomorrow, Friday, the ride ends.

Friday. We descend seven miles straight down, destined for the Lolo Pass some one hundred miles from where we started five days ago.

The land is, well, the land: vast beyond description, alive, ancient. The land is bigger than the lumber companies that methodically raze thousands of forested acres annually. It is bigger than the big flatbed trucks that carry the logs. It is bigger than the chain saws that rip through the wood, and it's bigger than the big men who use them. The land is bigger than the 400 colorful horses raising dust today on the dry trail. The land is so big that even if you are the last one to pitch your tent at the end of the day, you can still spread out on a good spot close to running water with giant pines protecting you like imposing night watchmen and a sapling right handy for hitching your horse. This ain't no franchise KOA Campground, pardner!

Roger has been following me around every day, demonstrating an almost clairvoyant ability to find me among any of 400 people at any given time. By Friday night, he waxes aloof. He retires to his tent early with a curt "Good night." His movements are unpredictable and jarring.

Saturday morning I wake, watchless, in the gray dawn. It must be early. Not many people stir. Horses paw and nicker as if they know they will be munching alfalfa tonight in their own barns. I slip over to where Joe is tied and ride him bareback to the river for water.

I have been with Joe now all week. I know when he is tired. I know what he likes to eat. He has shown me the kind of courage and gentleness that horse breeders call heart. I have done things with Joe that I haven't done since I was a kid, like ride bareback in the evenings with just halter and lead rope. I move to his movements without thought. I have been here before. It is all so natural.

As Joe gulps the good water, I straddle his warm back drinking in my last morning in the mountains, my last morning with Joe. Brushing his neck, I say good-bye to my gray friend with the hairless tail who has brought me home.

Roger ignores me at breakfast. He feigns surprise when he sees that I am standing right in front of him in line. I sit next to him, recalling a similar silent cowboy taking leave for no apparent reason nine years ago. "What is going on?" I ask.

"Nothing," Roger answers. "Everything is just fine."

And everything *is* just fine. I just got a second chance. Only this time the Marlboro man didn't make it in real life and saying good-bye was easy. And I got to fall in love again—with a horse—and say a proper good-bye. I got to embrace what nourishes me most—the land, the community, and most particularly, my own knowing. I am retuned again to someplace as familiar as my soul's bones. From now on, I would always be home.

The only people I find who will be passing through Minneapolis and have room for a passenger are two good old boys from Tennessee. "We'll be glad to take ya, Honey," the short one smiles, licking his lips. Sometimes it's not what you say, it's what you don't say. I decline the offer. I am glad to hear the man from Kentucky who was selling hats the first day has been busy scouting around for me. He needs to catch a plane in Lewiston. If I don't catch a ride to Minneapolis in someone's car, I too will have to catch a plane in Lewiston. There is only room for one person to ride back to Lewiston with the ride secretary and her husband. Therefore, the man from Kentucky has a vested interest in procuring a ride for me. He strikes pay dirt. Excited, he finds me packing up my tent.

"There's a couple from Ohio heard tell there's eagles nesting up in northern Minnesota. They want ta take a look. They got room fer ya. I b'lieve Cowhick's the name. Ya know 'em?"

Charlie is rearranging the family albums, all his souvenirs (including the six red-brimmed adjustable Chief Joseph caps), the pink and white striped canvas Cowhick family tent, the dog food, Betty's fine array of Liqui-Tex tubes, and all their John Wayne cassettes to make room in his homemade trailer for my gear. I crawl into the back seat of the Land Rover with their little German Shepherd, exhausted. Charlie's smile is almost as wide as the whole Bitterroot Valley.

"Betty Lou," he says, "those shorts yore wearin' today are pretty hot stuff. You better watch yourself around me, hear?"

He seems to feel her brown oxfords and ankle socks only add to the fashion statement.

Betty laughs, catching a wayward strand of hair in a bobby pin and at the same time elbowing Charlie, a "you fool" look in her eyes. Charlie checks the road conditions on his CB. We pull out onto 12, headed east for a KOA.

Yup. I know 'em. We're all a part of this going home thing. And it ain't half bad once you get the drift of it.

Bitterroot Blues

Finding Your Stories

1. Sometimes the road we travel is not on the AAA itinerary we took along. Things clear up while we're away. We are lulled by the clackety-clack of the train beneath us, and we know what we need to say to our lover. The future of our business becomes clear as we marvel at the Arizona desert in bloom. In the outhouse, we understand something fundamental about community. Tell about a trip that became a soul journey.

2. Start a sentence with "Going home is . . ." Write this sentence over and over, ending it with whatever comes to mind. Fill at least one sheet of paper. Write quickly and do not stop writing until you have filled at least one page. If your pen wants to carry on, let it. This exercise is a trip of sorts. See where it takes you.

3. Tell a story about someone you think is a little bit odd. Tell a story about someone you think is just about perfect. Toward whom do you gravitate? What draws you to them?

4. Tell about an incident that was like a rerun of a previous situation in your life. How was it the same? How was it different? How did you respond to the prospect of reexperiencing something you had already experienced? Did the rerun have a different ending? Why or why not?

5. It was a paradox for me to be in the heart of Indian country, commemorating the Nez Perce ordeal, and to have Janet and her husband complain about the Indians. Tell about a paradoxical situation you have been in. Did you want to take sides or did you dwell in the paradox? Tell the story both ways, even if only one is "The Truth."

My Legs Are Fine, the Boots Don't Fit

t took a good half-hour to get breakfast each morning, standing in the chow line with 400 horse lovers chomping at the bit to ride out by eight. However, the mountain vistas were better than any restaurant views, and I got to gabbing with the people in front of me and behind me, so the wait wasn't bad. We were on the Chief Joseph trail ride in the Bitterroot Mountains in Idaho. Five grand and glorious days of dusty roads and winding trails through virtually untamed wilderness. Cook tents were set up morning and night to feed the hungry riders.

One morning, as the breakfast line snaked its way to the griddle, we began talking about cowboy boots. On that ride we wore them all day and danced in them until way after the moon rose and the stars came out. They were the essential accoutrements. The tapered toe makes it easy to slip into the stirrup. The higher heel keeps the foot from accidentally slipping through the stirrup and hanging the rider up by the ankle. The upper protects the ankle from twisting and the leg area from snakebites and other hazards. Whether they are basic $75 Acmes or $900 custom-made kangaroo-skin, boots are expected to be at once practical, comfortable, and fashionable. Most people on a ride like this wore something in between, and fit was everything.

Sam stood in line in front of me, but backed through it most of the way to the cook tent because we were on a subject that rattled his sensibilities. He wanted to look us in the eye as he spoke. He was short enough that when I stood in front of him and looked straight ahead, I could see the whole Bitterroot Valley. But widthwise, he obliterated my view of three strapping white pines. He liked to eat, and this ride was no exception. His complaint was about boot tops.

"Now I got a big calf," he explained. "A lotta leg on me. The problem with boots is, they just don't make 'em big enough to fit my leg. Way too narrow for a guy like me. What do they expect me to do? Boot manufacturers should wake up and smell the coffee. Lotta guys like me out there." He pulled up his pant leg and showed us how his snug boot had rubbed the hair right off his meaty calf. The longer he went on, the madder he got.

I got to thinking about Sam's way of looking at things. It had never occurred to me to yell at clothing manufacturers for failing to fit what I saw as my flawed body. Most of the women I know, myself included, strive to wear clothing and makeup that help us appear uniformly taut and seamless. I was trained to camouflage the parts that bulged, not to take them in my stride, and certainly not to draw attention to them by talking about them in public. After a lifetime of being exposed to perfect-woman images on television and in magazines, many of us feel we need all the help we can get! It never occurred to me to fault the manufacturers. They were helping me achieve the ideal.

I remembered trying on shoes at Roberts Shoe Store on Chicago Avenue in Minneapolis. When I ordered size 10, the shoe salesman brought out a couple of pairs of chunky oxfords and said, "Here you go, Cinderella." The woman next to me was trying on over-the-calf winter boots. She tugged fruitlessly at an elegant pair made of supple leather that were too narrow to go over her calf, while the salesman talked zippers and elastic inserts. "Of course you can't get anything quite as classy with a leg like yours," the salesman said. The woman looked at the floor and slunk out of the store empty-handed.

The message for a woman is to hide her body and apologize for it. Diet into that boot. Maybe the fat will come off the calf first. They didn't have calf girdles then; now they have body shapers that are somewhat like spandex pantyhose without the feet. Now you can control those calves!

Certainly Sam would never go the body shaper route. Clearly not the masculine thing to do. I liked his unabashed style, so opposite my own and so refreshing. Women of the world, unite. Here's a little tip from Sam: When it comes to being the size and shape you are, kick back and kick butt!

My Legs Are Fine, the Boots Don't Fit

Finding Your Stories

1. The myth of the fashion model, the seamless, perfect woman, is one of those stories that many women live, whether it be to resist it or play it out. Identify a myth you live. Is it a cultural myth? A family myth? A personal myth? These kinds of myths are rarely defined as stories. If they were, we could separate ourselves from them and choose whether to live them or not. Create a story that brings your myth alive with characters, place, setting, point of view. It can be from real life, like the story about the boots, or you can make it into a fairy tale with kings and queens, paupers and peasants. Or create a fable with animal characters.

2. Is there an item of clothing that has a story connected with it?

3. What people do you know who wear unique, funny, or unusual clothing? What is their story?

4. Take one of your stories and make one character come alive through your description of his or her clothing. For instance, if you had a detective like Columbo, the rumpled trenchcoat would be essential to the story. What might he have in his pockets? Are his shoes scuffed or polished? What kind of shoes does he wear? Socks? Hat? Where does he carry his badge?

Sit in a Chair

Diane was a free spirit who made up her own rules. She held down a variety of odd jobs, dated whom she wanted to date, and enjoyed a revolving parade of flamboyant roommates. She came and went as she pleased. Her radiant smile illuminated our lively discussions. Inside this quirky package lived a thoughtful and caring woman. I got to know her well during the years I cut her hair.

One of Diane's enthusiasms led her into the world of social work, which in turn led her into the world of academia. She undertook a master's program with typical relish and with atypical follow-through. After graduating with honors, she left her lover, left her apartment in Minneapolis, and accepted a position at Wilmar State Hospital, working with the mentally ill. Wilmar is a prairie town two hours west of Minneapolis on Highway 12. It seemed like an idyllic place to Diane, a place to start a new life.

After she moved, I saw Diane only on her occasional trips to Minneapolis. She loved the slower pace of life in Wilmar. She had a great little house. She liked her job. She honed her tennis game with new friends. All in all, it was a good move.

But having a career was a new idea for Diane. She had prepared well for it academically, but she wasn't prepared for the daily demands on an overloaded staff or for the office politics. She took on more and more work and had less and less time. As the months passed, her rope got very short. Pretty soon she was at the end of it. She got upset easily. She was anxious about things that never bothered her before. She cried a lot. She began to see a therapist.

I came in on this story after Diane had spent several weeks sitting in a chair for an hour every day. During a haircut on one of her "city trips," I heard about what led up to her therapy and how, after assessing the situation, the therapist said, "Diane, here's what I want you to do. Just sit in a chair every day for an hour. That's all." So she did. And she was feeling much better.

I, on the other hand, couldn't digest this prescription. I like to keep busy. I like to have several projects going, several friends to talk to, several books to read at any one time. The idea of sitting in a chair was incomprehensible to me.

"Can you do anything while you're sitting there?" I asked.

"Oh, sometimes I fix a cup of tea and drink it," replied Diane. "Other than that, no."

"How can you sit and do nothing for an hour? Every day? I don't think I could do that," I said.

"I found it hard at first," Diane explained, "but then I began to look forward to it. Besides, I had to report back to my therapist, so I decided I'd better stick with it awhile."

"So what happens when you sit in a chair?" It seemed like pretty strange therapy to me.

"Things just sorted themselves out," Diane said. "Things that I felt bogged down about lightened up. I had set my needs aside as I tried to be my idea of a career person. Sitting in a chair put things in perspective. I started saying no to my boss about taking on more work." She became quiet, then continued.

"It changed how I dealt with time. I didn't think I had an

hour a day, but the hour a day gave me more time rather than less." She paused again, thoughtful.

"I saw situations for what they were. I became a person again, talking with other people, not a job description. I began to have fun again. And I learned to savor having time to myself."

"Wow," I said. "You got all that from sitting in a chair?"

"Yep." She seemed so peaceful.

I wanted some of that, but not enough to sit in a chair for an hour a day. I wondered how something that seems so simple could be so difficult for me. When my mother died several years later, I received her mint green, crushed velvet Queen Anne chair as a remembrance. I placed it in the corner of my loft bedroom by the east window where the sun washes in in the morning and where the moon mirrors the stars on clear nights. Maybe I will sit in it for an hour some day and see what happens.

Sit in a Chair

Finding Your Stories

1. Have you ever been strongly drawn to do something, but you resist doing it? What are you drawn to? What do you resist? What drew you to this activity in the first place? What are you afraid of? Make up a story about someone who does this thing and all your worst fears happen to that person.

2. Sit in a chair for fifteen minutes every day this week. (You can sit for an hour if you want to, but choose an amount of time you will actually spend. You don't have to start real big, just start.) Just sit there. At the end of the week, tell about your experience.

3. Have you ever been forced to *be*, not *do*? Recovering from a broken bone, being with someone who is dying, waiting for traffic to clear—those are being times. Recount a time when there was nothing more to do. What happened or didn't happen?

The Basketball Goddess

The day Dianne Goodwin got her new job as an engineer making devices for mentally and physically handicapped people was the day she discovered potter Barbara Hagar and began to collect her goddess pieces. At a local gallery store, she saw Barbara's laughing, joyous women flanked by dancing stars encircling large, sturdy, one-of-a-kind cups. The women on the cups reminded Dianne of the women at her new job. As a proclamation of new beginnings, she bought a cup for herself, a symbol of the future that was now possible. Still on her desk, the cup, as anticipated, is surrounded by good women and filled every day with savory tea and beauty.

"Barbara does goddess work," said Dianne. "She depicts joyful women with all different body shapes, lively men, and magical critters. There is an eighteen-inch plate with a rabbit in midjump that I really admire. I just bought a new bowl with three women in the center who are playfully connected and who obviously love one another." Her description of the new plate reminded me of the women in the creativity group that Dianne and I are a part of and the spirit of delight that is present every time we are together.

It was holiday time again, and Dianne started her shopping in Barbara's living room. Cups, bowls, pots, and vases crafted lovingly throughout the year adorned tables and displays. Every piece had a story. Dianne stood studying the intricacies of a twelve-inch goddess vase. She noticed that the face looked like the Queen of Hearts in a deck of cards; the skirt had deep pleats, and at the base of the skirt were swimming, leaping fish. "There was an inscription under the fish," reported Dianne. "I was standing there chuckling to myself, trying to read it—something irreverent, having to do with being on Prozac."

Just then, Barbara interrupted Dianne's reverie. "My

daughter Jenny has things for sale in the kitchen." Jenny is six. "Would you like to go look? Each of her pieces has a story, too, and she will gladly tell you the details if you ask." Dianne followed Barbara to the kitchen. Jenny had quite a collection, maybe twenty-five clay shapes all told, artfully arranged on the counters and table. "A big brown thing caught my eye," recounted Dianne. "It had an interesting form to it. I asked Jenny what it was."

"It's a woman," replied Jenny with assurance. "That's the head," she said, pointing to a tiny lump on the end. The head had a hole in it, as if hollowed out with a pencil.

Dianne turned it over. "What's this?" she said, pointing to a pinched-together mass in the clay. "Oh, she has a long braid down her back," beamed Jenny. "Of course," thought Dianne. There were two holes where the breasts might be, lines across the belly that Dianne thought looked like stretch marks, and another hole that was either the belly button or the vagina. "This is called 'Woman with Braid'," said Jenny. "And this goes with it."

She picked up a round, brown piece of clay, "about the size of a moose turd," in outdoorswoman Dianne's estimation, with lines carved on it. "And what is this?" Dianne inquired.

"It's a basketball," explained Jenny, matter-of-factly. There was a price tag on the bottom that Dianne couldn't quite read. "How much is it, Jenny?" she asked, definitely interested. How often do you find a woman with a braid who comes with her own basketball?

When Dianne and I were little girls, we wondered why they used "he" and "him" to mean everybody, why we couldn't be altar boys or play in the little leagues. Our mothers told us that was just the way it was. Besides, little girls were told that "he" meant "she" too—women really were included. We just had to understand that.

We understood that women were not included. We understood that women were not associated with basketballs.

"Seven cents," said Jenny.

Dianne had to have it. She reached into her pocket, found the seven cents, and took her new treasure home where it commands a special spot under the stained glass window in her front hall.

"Jenny had placed the basketball next to the woman, but I've laid it in the dent under her breasts. It's all pretty much in a lump, but it has a really good feel to it," says Dianne, smiling. "I call her 'The Basketball Goddess'."

The Basketball Goddess

Finding Your Stories

1. Sometimes simply using another sense gives rise to new stories. Take a lump of clay. Make a shape. Make up a story about it. This is a_____. You use it for____. It has seen____. If you knew what it knows, you would____. Keep going. Let a story unfold.

2. Give a lump of clay to a child. Have him or her make something from it and tell a story about it. Listen for leaps of imagination, detachment from doing it "right." Ask if you may join in. Trade clay objects and make up new stories.

3. Go out and shoot some hoops. Use your body. Do something completely physical. What story does your body want to tell?

4. Tell about an unusual place to shop.

5. Dianne's cup generated a series of events that built into a story. Take an object that means something to you and tell how it came

into your life, what it means to you, how you take care of it, where you put it, where it has taken you.

Zen and the Use of
Toilet Paper

Shoulder to shoulder, inquiring students sat cross-legged on round, black floor pillows, facing the white walls of the Minnesota Zen Meditation Center. We were there for an evening introduction to Zen. After a short lesson on how to arrange ourselves for sitting, at 7:30, without fanfare, three bells rang for zazen, or meditation time.

For the next twenty minutes we sat in silence, eyes open slightly, hands folded loosely at our diaphragms. During that time, we thought thoughts, heard noises, experienced our hands or feet going to sleep; we went to sleep, got bored, got agitated, got relaxed, got disgusted, got blissful, cynical, cold, hot, and back around again.

At the end of zazen, three bells rang again. We unfolded creaking knees as best we could from our formal sitting positions. A small, twinkling Japanese man in simple brown robes stepped into the room and invited us to gather for a brief talk and a time to ask questions. He settled easily onto his black pillow in front of a carved statue of the Buddha. We reconfigured our pillows and sank down on them once again, this time sprawling this way and that on the floor before Katagiri Roshi, the resident teacher and abbott of the Zen Center.

People asked all kinds of questions about Buddhism, none of which I can remember, save one. Katagiri called on a dark-haired man with a razor haircut, khaki dockers, and a red Polo sweater worn over a crisp, white oxford shirt, who was impatiently waving his hand in the air.

"Tell me," demanded the man. "I want to know, if I do this zazen, what will it get me? I want to know what the goal is. Where are we going with this?"

"Ah, yes," responded Katagiri in his Japanese accent.

"Hmmm." He closed his eyes, thought a moment, then continued.

"You know when you sit on toilet?"

I'd been daydreaming and this woke me up. "Before you do zazen you puulll toilet paper off roll." Katagiri made a fast sweeping gesture with his arm. "After zazen, you just take what you need." He folded his hands on his lap. "Next question."

The man in the red sweater did not find this sufficient incentive to take up Zen. I never saw him again. But it was a profound moment for me. Zen is simply life living itself in the moment with awareness. It is engaging with what is in front of you.

It is toilet paper as teacher.

Zen and the Use of Toilet Paper

Finding Your Stories

1. Make a power pouch of cloth or leather, and fill it with everyday things that remind you of the sacredness of life. Tie it with a ribbon or a leather thong, and wear it around your neck. Tell the story of what each object inside means to you.

2. Who or what reminds you to pay attention? How?

3. What do you really need? Take a moment and list those things. How much is enough?

4. Tell about a person you know who inspires you. What is one particular detail that creates a sense of who this person is?

5. Tell about a person you have read about or heard about who inspires you.

For information on personal coaching and/or workshop
offerings, please contact:

Lynn Baskfield
Coaching for Conscious Living
612-823-7022
coachlynn@mn.rr.com
Or visit www.creativecoaching.com

The Rakhma Story:

Unconditional Love and Caring
for People with Alzheimer's Disease and Dementia

by Shirley Joy Shaw as told to Lynn Baskfield

- Sets forth a dignified heart-based model of long-term care that works well for people with Alzheimer's disease and their families.
- Provides information about Alzheimer's care issues such as family decision making and response to memory loss.
- Sustains a model adaptable to other long-term care settings for the general elderly population.

ISBN 1-880090-83-X
quality softcover
$16.95
6 x 9
224 pages